PHILANTHROPY
AT
INDEPENDENT SCHOOLS
SECOND EDITION

Helen A. Colson

NATIONAL ASSOCIATION OF INDEPENDENT SCHOOLS

ISBN 1-893021-52-1

Printed in the United States of America

The National Association of Independent Schools represents 1,009 independent private schools in the United States in addition to 91 English-speaking schools in other countries. All are accredited, non-discriminatory, nonprofit organizations governed by independent boards of trustees.

NAIS's mission is to serve and strengthen member schools and associations by "articulating and promoting high standards of educational quality and ethical behavior, to work to preserve their independence to serve the free society from which that independence derives; to advocate broad access for students by affirming the principles of diversity, choice, and opportunity."

To find out more information about NAIS, go to *www.nais.org*. To receive a listing of NAIS books, call 1-800-793-6701 or 301-396-5911.

Book designer: Richard Fletcher
Editors: Karla Taylor, Nancy Raley

To the past and future students in my own family,
Adam, Amy, Eyal, Talia, Deborah, and Mark

CONTENTS

Introduction and Acknowledgements

It has been a pleasure and a challenge to write and to revise this book: a pleasure because I have enjoyed sharing my enthusiasm for independent school philanthropy and a challenge because I have tried to provide information of interest to both the beginner and the experienced professional.

This second edition includes much original text that has, happily, stood the test of time. I have added a new chapter on fund-raising policies and guidelines (Chapter Ten) and expanded the chapter on planned giving (Chapter Eight). Furthermore, every chapter contains new information and insights reflecting changes in the environment inside and outside independent schools during the past six years. Despite those additions, the book remains a slim volume in hopes of encouraging wide readership within development offices and among boards of trustees, school administrators, and fund-raising volunteers.

My focus continues to be on the principles, practices, and people directly involved in annual, capital, and planned gift fund raising. As a result, I have written little about alumni relations, publications, or special events. They are important topics but beyond the scope of this text.

I have attempted to convey my firm belief that fund raising is fun and those who devote themselves to independent school development—be they fund-raising professionals, school heads, trustees, or other volunteers—are a fortunate group. As they know, it is extraordinarily rewarding to bring together a generous donor and a worthy cause. The best development programs bring pleasure to all involved.

In addition, I have stressed my conviction that a successful development program must reflect the culture and climate of an individual school. In some respects, all well-run development programs are similar. Clearly it would be foolhardy to ignore proven techniques or to overlook significant trends. However, in many ways, the best programs differ. They are tailor-made to fit a school at a particular moment in its history and creatively designed to achieve distinct institutional goals.

I am deeply grateful to many talented independent school professionals who have provided valuable assistance during the writing of this book. For guidance as I wrote the first edition, I thank Curtis F. Baggett, John R. Barrengos, Mary Ann Bourbeau, Martha B. Bryans, Carolyn Burwell, Dwight D. Clasby, Margot Durkin, Nathan Follansbee, Earl G. Harrison Jr., Philip

Higginson, Virginia D. Howard, Patricia King Jackson, Richard K. Jung, Nancy Kami, Mary Louise Leipheimer, Carrie Levenson-Wahl, Michael J. Littell, Larry Lowenstein, Christopher A. Massi, Barbara F. Miller, Pat Morgan, John W. Moses, Mark H. Mullin, David G. Pond, Mary Reyner, Tracy G. Savage, Andrew B. Searle, Herbert P. Soles, Craig W. Stewart, Margery G. Topf, and Betsy H. Watkins. As a thoughtful reader, Lucy F. Leitzell did more than her share.

For help with the second edition, I turned to many of the same friends and colleagues listed above. Those who were kind enough to read and critique chapters once again include Virginia D. Howard, Patricia King Jackson, Lucy E. Leitzell, Tracy G. Savage, and Herbert P. Soles. For assistance with this second edition, I also thank Barbara Brown, Jean Waller Brune, Carolyn Christy, David Dini, Jay Goulart, Anne Seltzer, and Evelyn Zink.

It has been an honor to serve NAIS as a development consultant for the past 12 years. I have valued the colleagueship of many members of the NAIS staff. I am particularly grateful to Peter D. Relic, former president of NAIS, who believed in and promoted this project from the start; and to his successor, Patrick F. Bassett, who brings a wealth of development experience and expertise to his job. I also acknowledge the guidance of Jefferson G. Burnett, Brett Chambers, Margaret W. Goldsborough, James T. Kaull, and Donna M. Orem. Finally, I owe special thanks to three talented editors, Catherine O'Neill Grace, Nancy Raley, and Karla Taylor.

I am indebted to Millicent Adams Vesper, who has added her many skills to Helen Colson Development Associates for more than a decade. Finally, there is no way I can convey sufficient appreciation to my husband, Earl M. Colson, who has encouraged all of my professional activities for 40 years and who critically reviewed the tax and financial aspects of this text.

Although I benefited from the advice of all who are listed above, the opinions expressed in this book are my own. They are not necessarily those of the friends and colleagues who helped or of NAIS, the publisher of this text. The Reynolds School, which appears in charts and on forms, is a fictitious institution. School head Denise Harris, development director Fred Fiske, trustee Donald Green, and donors John and Mary Jones, Robert and Roberta Jones, and Sara Generous Jones are fictitious as well.

I hope that my belief in independent school education, my admiration for those who devote themselves to the welfare of independent schools, and my zest for the fund-raising challenges of pre-collegiate education are evident throughout this work. I will be content if readers are challenged to think about their own development agendas in new and creative ways.

Helen A. Colson
Chevy Chase, Maryland
February 2002

CHAPTER ONE

IN CHANGING TIMES
Constituents, Considerations, and Communication

First and probably foremost, a development department has to establish itself as the conscience of the institution, a voice that asks.... What are we selling to our donors?.... Do our potential giving publics perceive us in the same manner that we perceive ourselves?....Are the people in our institution behind our vision and do they understand the goals ahead?

—**How to Rate Your Development Office**
R.J. Berendt and J.R. Taft (Taft Group, 1983)

Independent schools have never had more to offer than they do today. Their curricula are creative and their community spirit is strong. Where else can one find a class small enough to provide individual attention but large enough to offer access, via the Internet, to knowledge throughout the world? What better enriches the education of all students than a school community reflecting the social, ethnic, racial, religious, and economic diversity of the planet on which its graduates will live?

Nevertheless, increased pluralism within the school and limitless access to information beyond its doors are presenting new challenges to those responsible for what is variously referred to as "development," "advancement," and "external affairs." For development officers, school heads, fund-raising volunteers, and trustees, there are new constituencies to understand and new capital needs to meet. And because there is increased competition for charitable gifts throughout the nonprofit world, there is new pressure to establish professional development programs and to recruit a top-notch staff.

Today, the leadership of independent schools is less insular and their major donors are more generous. Fortunately, high-net-worth individuals tend to be less affected by the ups and downs of the stock market when they make their giving decisions. These donors continue to give with increasing generosity to schools whose values they share, whose leadership they trust, and in whose future they are invested.

But never in recent decades have predictions about the future of philanthropy differed so significantly from publication to publication and even from day to day. Some experts say that an unsettled world and a volatile economy point to difficult challenges ahead for fund raisers. Others insist that the coming years hold great promise as a golden age of philanthropy.

One thing is certain: The trends listed on page three will have an impact on all fund-raising plans and programs.

FOUR PARENT GROUPS
Many of today's independent school families may not understand either the need for or the role of voluntary support.

There was a time when the majority of independent school parents understood the need for voluntary support. Many were habitual donors; some became significant philanthropists as well.

That time has passed. Today's parent constituencies reflect both the pluralism of the population nationwide and a determined effort on the part of schools to become more culturally, racially, religiously, and economically diverse. The face of independent school education has changed in important and positive ways. In response, development programs must change as well.

Many of today's independent school families may not understand either the need for or the role of voluntary support. In planning their fund-raising appeals, development officers should look carefully at the following groups.

1. The Public School Parent
First-generation independent school parents are increasingly prevalent at almost all independent schools. These parents attended public schools and believe in public school education. However, they have concluded that an independent school is a better option for their own children at this time.

Parents who attended public schools appreciate the academic excellence, the individual attention, and the safe and collegial environment of independ-

Continued on page 6

What 10 Trends Mean for School Fund Raising

Trend	*The Development Consequence*
1. Competition for gifts will increase. During the past 10 years, the number of nonprofit organizations seeking voluntary support has more than doubled. In the field of pre-collegiate education, many public school systems have established foundations through which they can seek gifts; the charter school movement, burgeoning in many cities, has added a new element of competition.	Independent school prospects are deluged with requests for support from worthy causes. Only through careful one-on-one nurturing of the individual major gift prospect will fund raisers be able to maintain the interest, involvement, and investment of those whose generosity can empower their schools.
2. Rapid technological change will continue. The technological revolution sweeping the globe is having a profound effect on all aspects of independent school education. Every year there are new options; for example, no sooner is an institution wired for the Web than it must consider becoming wireless. Networks and online communities are changing the way educators and fund raisers think, communicate, and solicit.	Schools will pay far more attention to the role of technology in general and to the quality and flexibility of their Web sites in particular. Publications, case statements, annual reports, and fund-raising updates will move to the Web. E-mail will be a key communication and solicitation tool, particularly for annual giving and for alumni relations. The development staff will devote much more staff time and money to learning about technology and using electronic communications.
3. Fund-raising potential will grow. During the next few decades, baby boomers (born between 1946 and 1964) will inherit many trillions of dollars from their parents. This will represent the greatest inter-generational transfer of wealth in history. In addition, younger philanthropists, particularly those who have enjoyed quick and remarkable business success, will offer generous support.	The schools that are best positioned to solicit six- and seven-figure gifts will: • research and cultivate the baby boomers and young philanthropists in their constituencies, • provide baby boomers with a wide range of planned gift vehicles, and • offer young philanthropists access to strategic plans and fiscal data. *Continued*

What 10 Trends Mean for School Fund Raising

Trend	*The Development Consequence*
4. Schools will rely more upon voluntary support. Always tuition-dependent, independent schools will have to continue increasing tuition annually to achieve programmatic and financial-aid goals. However, their financial pressures will increase because: • a nationwide teacher shortage will drive up salaries and benefits, • technology costs will be ongoing, and • both new facilities and repairs to aging physical plants will require substantial funding. As a result, the cost of education will grow beyond most schools' ability to increase tuition without putting it out of reach of the middle class. Voluntary support will, therefore, become even more important.	So that schools can fulfill their fund-raising potential, they will have to do a better job of funding and evaluating their development programs. They will focus more on fund-raising professionalism and expand their offerings to include annual, capital, and planned giving. The most professional programs will be geared to the needs and timetable of the major donor rather than to the school's fund-raising calendar. Major donor research, cultivation, solicitation, and stewardship will be ongoing priorities.
5. Strategic-planning cycles will grow shorter. The 10-year long-range plan is a dinosaur. In a fast-moving world where innovations in teaching and learning are continuous and the economy is unpredictable, it is impossible to think strategically and accurately about periods more than three to five years out—and even three- to five-year plans must be revisited and revised regularly.	Many schools will improve their governance structures to respond faster and more flexibly to emerging economic and educational issues. Schools will also increase efforts to build confidence in their fiscal decision-making and trust in their fiscal management. This will make them better able to attract unrestricted major gifts to meet unanticipated opportunities and needs.
6. The prospect pool will age. By the year 2020, 20 percent of Americans will be over the age of 65. Among them will be large numbers of independent school grandparents, parents of alumni, alumni, and even current parents.	Schools that wish to attract generous support from older donors will recruit them for boards and offer them leadership positions in their fund-raising efforts. Planned giving programs—especially those that offer donors over 65 the opportunity to increase retirement income, to pass assets on to another generation at lower cost, and to save or avoid taxes—will become more comprehensive and will be marketed with frequency and skill.

What 10 Trends Mean for School Fund Raising

Trend	The Development Consequence
7. More top philanthropists will be women. If the influx of women in the work-force was one of the most significant societal changes in the late 20th century, the rise of women to top positions may be among the most significant in the 21st. With increasing economic power will come increasing philanthropic importance. Women will play a substantially larger role in philanthropy, both as major donors and in high-profile fund-raising jobs.	It will be essential for independent school fund raisers to understand the approaches that work best for most women. For example, women often: • wish to be involved in the schools they support, • are encouraged by value-oriented causes, • want to know that their gifts are making a difference, and tend to be less influenced by pressure from peers.
8. Organized venture philanthropists will have an increasing impact. This will be the decade of the young high- tech entrepreneur, sometimes called the dot-com donor. Despite the continuing press coverage of failed high-tech ventures, many will succeed. The Web is here to stay, and so are those who find new and profitable ways to use it. High-tech investors of the future will continue to be mostly under age 40, well educated, and from diverse educational backgrounds. They also have little experience with philanthropy. In increasing numbers, they are becoming "venture philanthropists," merging their charitable resources and seeking professional advice about how best to use them.	The new nonprofit organizations created to guide the philanthropy of young high-tech investors will become more influential. These organizations have proliferated because young donors wish to become better educated about responsible philanthropy and to make grants with broad and significant impact. In particular, these venture philanthropists are interested in using business strategies to evaluate schools and to make them more effective. To appeal to venture philanthropists, schools should: • do careful fiscal planning, documentation, and evaluation; • have well-articulated strategic goals; and • offer fiscally oriented donor education in writing and on the Web.

What 10 Trends Mean for School Fund Raising

Trend	*The Development Consequence*
9. Hiring skilled development professionals will be a challenge. This is because of the increase in non-profit organizations seeking voluntary support and the increasing dependence upon charitable gifts within the independent school world. Hiring skilled directors of development, major gifts, and planned giving will grow both more difficult and more important.	Development salaries will increase, and development directors will be treated as senior members of the administration. These skilled fund-raising professionals will meet frequently with trustees, major gift solicitors, and major donor prospects. More and more often, development directors will help to solicit gifts.
10. The individual philanthropist will be carefully researched and nurtured. Although foundations and corporations will still support education, the generous individual donor will continue to provide the vast majority of total voluntary support. If recent trends continue, fewer and fewer of these individuals will make larger and larger gifts. Schools will typically depend upon 5 to 10 percent of their prospects to contribute 90 to 95 percent of their annual, capital, and planned gifts each year.	To meet their fund-raising potential, schools will focus vastly more professional and volunteer time on the research, cultivation, solicitation, and stewardship of major gift prospects from the past, present, and future. The entire development office staff will play a role in major gift fund raising. School heads and board members will better understand the key role major donors play and will devote more time to courting and appreciating them.

ent schools. But often they do not understand the economics of private-sector education. Because they are paying a substantial amount of tuition, they may believe that their school is rich, that its fiscal reserves are large, and that its teachers are well paid.

2. The Foreign-Born Parent

Urban day schools have more students whose parents have immigrated from abroad. Boarding schools have increasing numbers of students whose homes are in Europe, the Middle East, South America, and the Pacific Rim.

Many of these parents do not view their children's school as a charitable institution worthy of support. More typically, they feel they have a business relationship with the school, from which they are purchasing a service at its market value.

3. The Financial-Aid Parent

Throughout the independent school world, the number of parents benefiting from financial aid is increasing as well. In 2001-2002, many NAIS schools offered need-based aid to 20 percent of their families. At some schools the proportion is significantly higher than that; averages of 40 percent are no longer unusual at well-endowed institutions.

Parents who receive financial aid are less able to offer generous support. And why should they contribute, they may wonder, when it seems that many others in the school community can make large gifts without sacrifice?

4. The Consumer Parent

During decades past, many independent school parents were loyalists; they made gifts to preserve the attributes of schools that had often educated generation after generation of their kin. "Here, Mr. Headmaster," they would say. "Take my gift and use it as you think best."

Today's parents think more like consumers. They are making an investment, so they are interested in the nature and quality of the return. Often called "consumer parents," they seek evidence of a school's financial security and financial management skill. They focus on educational standards and test scores. They hold the school accountable for all that its mission statement and brochures promise it will do.

SEEKING SUPPORT FROM THESE GROUPS

Transforming some families into donors takes a thoughtfully planned curriculum and a talented teaching team.

These parents and their children, the future alumni of the school, can become philanthropists. At many institutions, they are offering unprecedented levels of support. However, this transformation requires a thoughtfully planned curriculum and a talented teaching team. The first step is to divide potential donors into separate groups with different orientations and views. For example, which parents attended public school? Which are foreign born? The second step is to educate each group as necessary and appropriate well before its members ever receive a fund-raising appeal. The annual giving solicitation that once came first now comes last. Before many of today's parents are ready to be asked for a gift, schools need to help them learn the following four important lessons.

Lesson 1: Philanthropy and the Nonprofit Sector

The prominence and stature of the nonprofit sector is a largely American phenomenon. In parts of the world from which increasing numbers of independent school students come, there is little tradition of philanthropy as understood in the United States.

Therefore, for some parents, the fund-raising education must begin with Philanthropy 101: the importance of the independent sector and the role it plays in promoting choice, innovation, and excellence. Often parents from abroad who send their children to independent schools have the ability to make major gifts. However, first they must understand that philanthropy (voluntary action for the public good) is essential in a democratic society and key to excellence at independent schools.

Lesson 2: The Mission of the School

Parents unfamiliar with independent education may not understand many schools' deep commitment to a value-centered curriculum that not only prepares students for college but also teaches them to respect those who think differently and inspires them to help those who have been given less.

The institutional mission—to teach students to live fully and productively in a complex world with shrinking resources—is an important aspect of the fund-raising appeal. For many parents, the school's noble mission makes it worthy of philanthropic support.

Lesson 3: The Economics of Independent Education

Each school must tell its story to potential donors who do not understand the fiscal need. Here, for example, is the description offered by an urban day school:

> At our school, tuition provides 81.7 percent of total operating revenue. We don't want to increase the tuition way beyond the inflation rate each year because we don't want to polarize the student body between the rich, who can afford a high tuition, and the financially stretched, who qualify for financial aid. We feel responsible to the many middle-income families in our school.
>
> We budget financial aid at 10 percent of tuition revenue. That's because we value diversity; we believe that diversity of all kinds—including economic—enriches the education of all who attend our school.
>
> Please understand that we're a labor-intensive enterprise; we spend 75 percent of our revenue on the compensation of our faculty, administration, and staff. Even so, our average faculty salary is $47,000 this year, and that is paid to a teacher who is 38 years old and has been teaching for 15 years.

Lesson 4: The School's Need for Voluntary Support

To the development staff and volunteers, annual, capital, and planned giving are familiar concepts. However, many independent school constituents, parents, and grandparents in particular are completely unfamiliar with these fund-raising terms.

Therefore, before the annual appeal arrives, it is useful to provide an overview of the fund-raising agenda as a whole. Here's the message offered—both in writing and orally—to new parents at an elementary school:

> Every year we will ask you to make an annual gift. Through the annual generosity of our parents, grandparents, alumni, and parents of alumni as well, we raise 8 percent of our operating revenue. No gift is too large, but neither is any gift too small. We ask all parents to make an annual gift because a high participation rate helps us raise money from foundations that support independent schools.
>
> Once a decade, we have a capital campaign as well — to help us build new facilities and to increase our small endowment fund. All of the facilities that your son or daughter is enjoying have been made possible by those who responded in the past to our capital appeals. The largest single gift we have ever received is $1,000,000. We used that and other gifts to build the fine library that opened last year.
>
> We also offer the opportunity to make planned gifts from which donors often realize both increased income and tax savings. These planned gifts are current and deferred. Last year, for example, we received $400,000 in the form of bequests.

THE WELL-TAILORED GIFT REQUEST
An effective solicitation is specific, inspiring, and appropriate for the prospect.

Finally, it's time for the first gift request: the annual giving visit, letter, or call. That, too, should be specific and complete; it should both inspire and inform. Why is voluntary support needed this year and how will the gifts be used? How much has been raised in the past and with what size gifts? What is the annual giving timetable? What kinds of gifts qualify?

At many schools, staff or volunteers present the annual giving appeal to new parents in person to make sure they understand the lessons about philanthropy and to emphasize the importance the schools attach to voluntary support. In many instances, it is wise to communicate in the donor's first language; a letter or a conversation in Japanese or Spanish will be deeply appreciated and is more likely to provide the appropriate tone.

EVERYONE HAS A ROLE
Fund raising is an opportunity to educate.

But a school's fund-raising curriculum cannot be taught by the development staff alone. All administrators should play a role.

For the admissions office staff, the opportunity to educate comes first. Both printed viewbooks and oral presentations should include information about the importance of charitable giving, including its role in providing capital improvements and ongoing operating revenue. Furthermore, the application itself should be designed to yield information of potential importance to the development staff, such as the parents' alma maters, the names and addresses of grandparents, and the mother's maiden name.

The school head should be sensitive to the many opportunities to teach all constituents about the need for voluntary support and about the role of major gifts in the future welfare of the school.

Finally, trustees and volunteers have a special part to play as mentors of constituents new to independent schools. The more individually and personally these newcomers are welcomed at the start, the deeper their interest and involvement are likely to be.

LITERATE COMMUNICATION COUNTS
Five rules that can help.

Throughout the development process, literate communication counts. In an independent school that emphasizes high standards of writing in the classroom, the development office's publications, proposals, newsletters, letters, and other written communications must meet high standards. What do parents or alumni think when they receive a letter or newsletter whose text would receive a C in ninth-grade English?

Good writing for development begins with simple sentences. It is well organized and well proofread. It is fresh, warm, and sincere. It has a clear purpose and is appropriate for its audience.

Foundation proposals pose a particular challenge for many development staffs. The worth of an important school project is sometimes lost in a mass of verbiage. Here are some key points to consider in writing for development.

- *Do not cut and paste.* Taking a paragraph here and there from another fundraising letter or foundation proposal rarely works. Resist the temptation to save time this way. Such text does not flow smoothly. It is far better to outline and to write each document on its own.
- *Avoid using adjectives like "creative," "innovative," and "unique."* Instead, vividly describe the project or the need so that its creativity and unique qualities are clear.
- *Be consistent.* Be careful not to change the text at random from the third person ("the school") to the first person ("we") and then back again.
- *Be concise.* In particular, avoid repeating facts or ideas without amplification or purpose.

- *Proofread and proofread again.* Grammar and spellchecks on the computer are wonderful, but they do not catch everything. There is no substitute for careful rereading of the final proposal by two different people.

THE WONDERS OF THE WEB
In fund raising, the Web is a particularly effective tool.

No school can ignore the impact of the Web on education, communication, admissions, marketing, public relations, development, alumni relations, and much more. The Web is at once an expensive budget item and a great equalizer. Using the Web, the new small school has the same potential as the established large school to contact its constituency, to market its institution, and to reach a worldwide audience.

In major gift philanthropy, the Web is an essential tool for research, communication, cultivation, stewardship, and, in some cases, solicitation. Many young venture philanthropists prefer to communicate by e-mail.

However, it is important to remember that although "e-philanthropy"—the use of the Internet for fund raising of all kinds—may add effective new fund-raising techniques, it is unlikely to change the basic rules. Those schools that attract major gifts continue to focus on building close relationships with individual prospects in person and over time. The process of building trust between a school and a potential donor and the nurturing of a prospect's most generous support is assisted, but not short-changed or cut short, by electronic communication.

As more schools become aware of all that the Web can do and fully commit to underwriting the cost, its use for all kinds of fund raising will become more widespread and more effective. For example, a handful of boarding schools have individual Web pages for their top prospects. If the prospect's child scores a winning soccer goal, a photo of the moment is transmitted to a personalized Web page even before the proud athlete calls home. Now that's impressive cultivation—not in place of, but in addition to, face-to-face meetings.

As in many arenas of educational advancement, higher education is setting the pace in e-philanthropy. College and university Web pages already serve many functions and bring together numerous online communities. Most Web sites are well designed, well staffed, and in continuous evolution. They don't simply reproduce the mission; they represent it as well.

It is best for independent schools to approach their use of the Web for fund-raising and all other purposes by thinking big but starting small. Web pages are virtual communications; they must be kept up-to-date. It is far better to have a smaller, well-maintained site than a larger one that is static.

Launching a new site is expensive. It should be done only after a skilled, in-house Web manager is available to update the site and to track its use. The development staff will need to acquire additional expertise to manage those annual campaigns that rely upon e-mail for solicitation and stewardship. Electronic gift acceptance will require a secure server that can handle sensitive and confidential information.

Here is the challenge for the years to come. Independent schools must move slowly but steadily toward a full understanding of the best and most cost-effective uses of the Web for schools in general and e-philanthropy in particular, even as electronic communication's potential continues to grow at a remarkable pace.

CHAPTER TWO

THE DEVELOPMENT OFFICE PLAN

ORGANIZING FOR SUCCESS

*If you want people to be effective, you have to give them a structure.
There has to be a way to measure performance and result—something
against which to shine. Human beings need goals and deadlines. They
need to know what is expected of them, and where they fit into the
big picture.*

— The Raising of Money
James Gregory Lord (Third Sector Press, 1984)

Effective development professionals make plans. They set priorities and goals. They prepare budgets and track expenses. They understand the relationship between the resources they have (staff, space, information systems, money, etc.) and the fund-raising results they are likely to achieve. They track cost-effectiveness—the relationship between money spent and money raised.

Schools whose development programs are guided by concise, clear, written plans are most likely to fulfill their fund-raising potential. Furthermore, schools whose development directors think ahead are better able to anticipate and to manage change.

Most schools have development calendars. However, a calendar is only part of a plan. The calendar tells when something will be done and often by whom. The plan outlines why and how something will be done and with what intended result.

A MINDSET FOR THE NEW MILLENNIUM

Looking back, it is hard to believe that independent schools ever created 10-year development plans. However, that was the norm for decades.

In the 21st century, planning requires much more flexibility. Even a one- to three-year plan must be adjusted annually as the economy lurches, school leadership changes, tax-exempt bonds alter fund-raising initiatives, zoning appeals delay timetables, technological advances emerge, and changing demographics affect enrollment.

Planning has never been more important, but, at the same time, plans have never required more frequent review. To provide this monitoring, planners—be they trustees, school heads, or development directors—must be constantly on the alert and continually on the job. School budgets, campaign timetables, and investment policies are only a few of the issues subject to change. Strategic thinking and flexible planning have become essential.

THREE KEY DOCUMENTS

An independent school development program is supported by three documents.

1. *The institutional mission statement* tells what the school is trying to do, why, and for whom.
2. *The strategic plan* tells how the school plans to implement its mission during the next three to five years. It identifies institutional priorities and goals.
3. *The development plan* tells how and when the school will raise the money it needs to achieve these goals. The best development plans focus on both a one-year and a three-year horizon. They reflect the multiyear effort that goes into seeking a major gift.

As Robert J. Berendt and J. Richard Taft write in *How to Rate Your Development Office* (Taft Group, 1983), "It is a fact of life that development is a long-term enterprise where results can neither be anticipated nor evaluated quickly. Certain kinds of contributions may require years of cultivation before an actual cash commitment is made."

The best development plans also acknowledge that fund-raising programs are least cost effective at the start. As in most endeavors, an initial investment is required to begin.

"In a sense, the development function is like any business operation," James Gregory Lord states in *The Raising of Money*. "The greater risk for either enterprise is in the early years, when they are most vulnerable to the effects of undercapitalization."

TOO BUSY TO PLAN?

The development officer who's stretched too thin to plan needs a plan the most.

Many development directors—particularly those in small shops—question whether planning is worth the effort and the time. Here's a comment from one professional who oversees an office of two:

"Do you know what the two of us are expected to do? Annual giving and major donor research and cultivation in preparation for a capital campaign. Public relations, publications, special events, and the alumni program. And don't forget the meetings: the board, the development committee, the administrative staff, the alumni board, and the parents association. I have to attend them all and, when they're over, I always have something new to do. A development plan is a fine idea, but I can't fit it in. I already have too many demands and too little time!"

Ironically, he is the development officer who most needs a plan. A development planning process and a written development plan would help him prioritize the "too many demands" and better manage the "too little time." He would discover that planning moves a development program forward in the following significant ways:

It helps to set realistic fund-raising goals.

Unrealistic goals are based upon institutional needs alone. Realistic goals are based upon fund-raising potential as well. They take into account the various resources the school can bring to bear: people, money, systems, time. They acknowledge the level of staff experience and expertise.

It keeps staff and volunteers on schedule.

To achieve an annual giving goal by June, one must take certain steps each month. All development activities—from a small class reunion to a major capital campaign—are geared to a series of deadlines that should be spelled out in advance.

It helps to set program priorities.

Development directors receive urgent requests from many fronts. However, only so many program initiatives are feasible in any one school year.

Development directors who have set program priorities are able to focus on the most important work.

It clarifies fiscal needs and keeps programs cost-effective.

Development planning includes a careful look at the relationship between resources spent and money raised. It helps the staff keep track of costs and relate them to results. It focuses attention on percentages of growth by program and constituency and from year to year. Often the planning process helps the development director make an effective case for getting a bigger budget and a larger staff.

It helps the director delegate tasks.

A development plan leads to more effective delegation to both staff and volunteers. It encourages staff members to assume more personal responsibility for their work because they better understand that the development director can't manage it all.

It helps to ensure a fair evaluation of program and staff.

When the board, the school head, and the development director agree on goals and priorities in advance, a year-end evaluation is likely to be more productive, useful, and fair.

It educates key administrators and involves key prospects and volunteers.

Participation in planning leads to a proprietary interest in results. The more fully the school head and board understand the development challenges, the more helpful and supportive they will be. The same is true of fund-raising volunteers. The more major prospects are involved in the planning process, the better they will understand the urgency of the need and the importance of their generous support.

It ensures that the program will become more professional each year.

Too many independent school development programs maintain the same level of professionalism each year. They may raise slightly more money, but they do not increase their sophistication or scope. Development planning forces a look at fund-raising concepts as well as fund-raising techniques. It focuses on fund-raising potential as well as fund-raising results. It is geared to tomorrow as well as to today.

THE PROCESS: WHO, WHAT, AND WHEN

A good plan makes every season of the year more productive.

Development planning is a team effort led by the development director, school head, and development committee chair. Among the planners are staff and volunteers who will be responsible for implementing the plan, key volunteers who will solicit gifts, and major prospects who have the ability to help the school achieve its fund-raising goals.

Many development professionals begin in January to plan for the following school year. Therefore, they are well positioned to recommend or to react to a proposed annual giving goal before it becomes a line item in the next year's budget. By May, the school has set its fund-raising priorities and the development deadlines and goals for the upcoming school year. In July, the staff can make adjustments based upon the current year's fund-raising results. All of this helps the development office guard against:

1. **Overscheduling**—planning too many mailings or events in any one month or asking the school head to do too much during January, February, and March, which are often his or her busiest times of the year.

2. **Poor timing**—scheduling a fund-raising event during the same week the annual appeal is mailed or sending an annual giving reminder on the day the second semester bill is mailed.

Furthermore, planning makes it possible for the summer to be productive. Members of the staff can use that time to recruit annual giving chairs and committees. They can prepare annual giving brochures. They can compose annual giving letters, even those to be mailed many months hence. They can print pledge envelopes. And they can set phonathon dates.

Then the development staff can spend the fall implementing rather than making fund-raising plans, working with rather than forming annual giving committees. Beginning in September, the annual giving program can focus on people rather than on paper and on soliciting promising donors rather than composing mass appeals. The staff has time during the school year to cultivate top prospects, to create strategies for individual gift requests, and to evaluate progress along the way.

The following sections spell out important components for short-term, long-term, and personal plans, all of which are vital to fund-raising success.

THE SUBSTANCE: A ONE-YEAR HORIZON

Annual plans usually include both development basics and three or four priorities for growth.

The most effective short-term plans cover these elements.

- *Money:* How much will we seek in total voluntary support?
- *Sources:* From which constituencies will these funds come?
- *Goals:* What results—both short and long term—should each drive—annual, capital, and planned giving—achieve?
- *Top prospects:* How will our major donor research, cultivation, and stewardship efforts proceed?
- *Community outreach:* What are our plans in the areas of alumni relations and community events?
- *Communication:* What messages will we stress in publications and institutional publicity this year?
- *Personnel:* How will we assure our staff's professional growth and effective management of our volunteers?
- *Office:* How can we improve our development systems and office management techniques?

Usually development plans also highlight three or four areas for particular growth or change. These become top priorities for the development office staff, programs, or projects on which they focus throughout the school year.

For example, at one large independent day school, the planners have identified the two following priorities (each with implementation strategies) for the upcoming school year.

1. At the board's request, the development staff and volunteers will aim for a significantly higher annual giving goal.

Mature annual giving programs (those in which all gifts and grants, restricted and unrestricted, are donated to support current operations) typically raise 8 to 10 percent of annual operating revenue. At many schools, this percentage is much lower; at others, it is as high as 12 to 15 percent. At this school, the board wishes to increase annual giving revenue from 6 to 8 percent of operating revenue in one year, a particular challenge since the budget itself is increasing by 3 percent.

To achieve this result, the members of the planning committee have come up with five new ideas:

- A board challenge to be met by new and increased gifts.
- A higher top gift club—up from $5,000 to $10,000.
- A new gift club for donors who increase their previous gifts by 20 percent.

- A major gifts committee that will solicit 50 top prospects face to face.
- An expanded alumni phonathon with better training for volunteers.

2. The school will attempt to develop closer ties to particular top prospects.

These prospects are the ones who have the capacity to make leadership gifts but who are not yet well informed about the institution's needs or personally invested in its success.

The planners have designed a weekend program called "A Close and Personal Look," a small cultivation event for 25 top prospects who are not currently involved in school affairs. The program is to include individual visits to classes of the visitors' choice, a planned giving seminar, and a dinner with the headmaster and board at a nearby historic home. It will coincide with the annual fall concert and fair.

After the weekend, the school will make a special effort to stay in close touch with those who attend. Each will be assigned to an individual cultivator who will make sure that there is one personal contact each month—activities as simple as a note from the headmaster attached to the annual report or a special invitation (with tickets enclosed) to the spring musical. If this new method of cultivation is successful, the school will continue to use it with additional prospects in subsequent years.

THE SUBSTANCE: A THREE-YEAR HORIZON

Long-term plans can be—and should be—more ambitious.

Development plans often include longer-term goals that the school intends to achieve within three years. These goals may relate to changes in staff size or office technology, items that necessitate good planning because they are costly. Often, long-term goals also focus on major gifts and the programs to achieve them, be they occasional capital campaigns or ongoing efforts to solicit planned gifts.

Major donor research and cultivation is both a challenge for the present and an investment in the future. As John R. Chandler wrote in *A Development Handbook: Promoting Philanthropy at Independent Schools* (CASE, 1992), it is important that every school "incorporate in its development strategy an ongoing program focusing on those relatively few donors who have the resources to make significant major gifts that determine the school's future."

At the independent school mentioned above, the following three long-term priorities have been set. The first focuses on major prospects within the context of a planned giving review.

1. A Fresh Look at Planned Giving

This school launched a planned giving program six years ago. A comprehensive review seems timely.

The school's planned giving committee will be asked to evaluate the results to date. How much cash has been received and how much is committed but deferred? Is the five-year-old Bequest Society attracting more members each year? What new planned gift vehicles should be introduced in the years to come? Finally, is the program promising enough to warrant the addition of a full-time planned giving officer?

2. A Review of the Alumni Program

A second priority with longer-term consequences is a review of the alumni relations program and *The Quarterly Report*, the school's magazine for alumni and friends. A review is appropriate since one-third of the school's alumni have graduated during the past 10 years. It is wise to consider the particular program interests of these younger alumni as well as ways to encourage their more generous support.

An ad hoc committee of 10 alumni has been formed to undertake this task. They will begin their work by sending a survey to the school's 3,000 alumni. The committee will also look at alumni programs at similar schools. Finally, they will evaluate *The Quarterly Report* to determine how it might better represent the school's historic mission and present strengths.

The ad hoc committee has been asked to submit a written report in the spring. Its suggestions will be shared with the administration, the development committee, and the board.

3. Looking Ahead to the Centennial Year

Finally, it is important to anticipate the centennial year five years hence. What kind of celebrations will be most effective? Should the school commission a centennial history? How might the centennial attract widespread and positive publicity? What impact should it have on annual and capital fund-raising drives? It is not too soon to consider such an important moment in the history of the school.

A small group of staff and volunteers has been asked to begin this study and to come up with a preliminary plan by the end of the academic year.

THE PERSONAL PLAN

In addition to planning the development program with care, every development director also needs to create a personal plan. That plan answers questions like these:

- Which programs and staff members most need my personal attention?
- How can I work more effectively with my school head, trustees, and fund-raising volunteers?
- How can I improve my fund-raising knowledge and skills?
- If I leave this job in a year, will my program and my insights be documented in good computer records and files?

Often, development directors share some of these goals with their school heads to assure mutual understanding and to guide them to a productive year-end performance review.

It's no surprise that schools with development plans have greater fund-raising success. Nor is it a surprise that they have happier development directors as well. With a road map to follow, every professional is more likely to reach his or her destination both in good spirits and in good time.

Fund-Raising Results:
How Much and Compared to Whom?

"I just received an annual report from my other child's school. Why does it raise so much more money than we do?"

Too many development directors hear that question every year.

Sometimes comparing one school's fund-raising results with another is appropriate, but often it is not. Two schools in the same city and of similar size may achieve significantly different fund-raising results. One, for example, may have alumni who are older, who are more numerous, and who have multigenerational ties. One school's parents may be more accustomed to philanthropy, and the trustees' development roles may be better defined. Furthermore, its development program may be well established and more generously funded, and its staff larger and better trained.

When fund-raising comparisons are made with other schools, they should be on the basis of funds raised per student and improved results from year to year, rather than on the basis of total funds raised in a particular year. Via its StatsOnline service, NAIS offers members the ability to access this type of data and develop customized reports that permit schools to compare themselves with selected institutions and in appropriate ways.

In addition, the national summaries by NAIS and the Council for Aid to Education are helpful in identifying averages, ranges, and trends. However, it is not fair to use them in isolation to make a particular development office (or officer) look good (or bad). There are simply too many other factors at play.

The most useful comparisons of fund-raising results are with past performance at one's own school. Development directors should ask themselves the following six questions every year.

1. Are we raising both more money and an increased percentage of operating revenue each year?
2. Are we adding significantly to our donor pool?
3. Has the average annual gift increased?
4. Are we using effective research to increase our prospect base?
5. Are we focusing enough of our attention on major prospects and major gifts?
6. Are we spending too much time or money relative to the amount we raise?

(Regarding development costs: The Council for Aid to Education reports that the average total development expense at independent schools that respond to its annual survey has remained steady at 4 percent of total school expense during the past decade. Development expense includes total staff compensation and the entire range of advancement activities, including alumni relations, special events, and publications.)

The following sample plan, used by a fictitious school in the final year of a capital campaign, illustrates a useful planning format. For each of the goals that follow, there is also an implementation strategy and a designated staff member responsible for implementation. (Other schools considering this as a model should keep in mind that undoubtedly the substance of their plans will differ.)

THE REYNOLDS SCHOOL'S DEVELOPMENT PLAN

Goal 1: To raise donor sights through leadership giving

- Solicit all remaining capital campaign leadership prospects for gifts of at least $10,000.
- Solicit all previous annual giving donors of $500 and above (who have not been approached during the capital campaign) for gifts of at least $1,000.
- Ask all previous annual giving donors in the leadership category for increased gifts.
- Add 100 donors to the top annual giving gift club.

Goal 2: To increase the donor base

- Seek 100 percent support from senior-class parents.
- Increase annual giving donor pool by 10 percent.
- Increase alumni participation to 45 percent.
- Increase parent participation to 95 percent.
- Successfully seek gifts from 100 SYBUNTS.
- Achieve five new foundation grants.
- Offer donors who have made multi-year annual giving pledges during the campaign the opportunity to continue multi-year pledging.

Goal 3: To increase total voluntary support for the school

- Achieve annual giving goal of $1,000,000.
- Complete capital campaign by raising additional $5,000,000 in pledges and gifts.

Goal 4: To increase levels of professionalism and efficiency within the development office

- Review goals and objectives quarterly.
- Evaluate program at year-end.
- Send each staff member to one conference that he or she will summarize in writing for the entire staff.
- Update the job description for each staff member.
- Institute a policy for dealing with the media and key constituencies in a crisis situation.
- Develop a five-year plan for equipment upgrade.
- Upgrade the computer literacy of each staff member.

Goal 5: To communicate effectively with the entire constituency

- Publish magazines in September, January, and April.
- Publish campaign newsletters in November and May.
- Communicate regularly by e-mail with annual giving volunteers, alumni class secretaries, the alumni board, and the board of trustees.
- Publish a new school calendar featuring student art.

Goal 6: To provide high-quality cultivation activities

- Host four regional reunions.
- Publish a directory for alumni in college.
- Institute an alumni internship program in the development office.
- Create two new events for young alumni.
- Continue to upgrade existing alumni events.
- Identify additional school events that might benefit from alumni involvement.
- Evaluate the establishment of a board of visitors.
- Organize weekly headmaster lunches with top prospects.
- Organize one personal cultivation contact per week for each member of the development staff.

Goal 7: To recognize and appreciate donors and volunteers

- Publish an annual report in October.
- Invite all $10,000 and above donors to a November party.
- Invite all fund-raising volunteers to an appreciation party in December.
- Send leadership donors a gift from the headmaster during the holidays.
- Send leadership donors a written report on the use of their gifts.

Goal 8: To create a new stewardship program

- Describe the program in writing.
- Assign roles to staff members, headmaster, and trustees.
- Develop a system for monitoring and evaluating success.

Goal 9: To better articulate the role of development within the school

- Share weekly development staff meeting minutes with headmaster.
- Send one development staff member to each faculty meeting.
- Send each development staff member to one non-development school activity per week.
- Send a development representative to each parents association meeting.
- Send an annual letter to faculty regarding development program.
- Make two oral presentations on development program to the faculty each year.
- Make two oral presentations on development program to the alumni board each year.

CHAPTER THREE

THE BOARD'S ROLE IN DEVELOPMENT
THE QUERY OF DONALD GREEN

"When I joined this board, nobody said a thing about giving money or asking others to give. The board chair said he'd be honored to have me serve and I said I'd be honored to accept. Now we're launching a capital campaign and I'm told that it's my responsibility as a trustee to make an 'early sacrificial gift.' Am I the only one who thinks that's adding some rules in the middle of the game?"

Donald Green, a parent and trustee at an independent school, asked this question at a September meeting of his board. The school's director of development, Fred Fiske, replied, "Trustees are the school's leaders. Giving and raising money are among the most important ways in which they lead. I've been assuming everybody knew that."

However, as the subsequent discussion revealed, everybody did not know that. Many other trustees agreed with Donald Green that their general role in development was unclear and their philanthropic responsibilities in particular were unspoken, unwritten, and vague.

Similar situations exist at many independent schools. The board avoids defining philanthropic responsibilities in an effort to make every trustee feel welcome and valued, regardless of his or her ability to provide generous support. However, as Donald's reaction suggests, this lack of forthrightness about the board's giving-and-getting role creates the very feelings of discomfort it is intended to avoid.

In fact, those independent school boards that candidly discuss and clearly define their development roles are the most successful at making all trustees comfortable about philanthropy.

During the past decades, more and more independent school boards have drafted trustee job descriptions that explicitly define expectations about development and philanthropy. These descriptions, which are shared with prospective trustees during the recruitment process, have become prevalent as boards have grown more conscientious about reflecting their schools' economic diversity.

On an economically diverse board, it is the **nature** rather than the **amount** of the trustee contribution that is appropriately defined. The key elements of trustee philanthropy are "unanimity of response at an obviously sacrificial level," as Harold Seymour wrote in *Designs for Fund-Raising* (Taft Group, 1999)—still a timely text more than 35 years after it was first published.

THE TRUSTEE GIFT
Independent school trustees must be philanthropic pacesetters during a capital campaign.

During a subsequent board retreat devoted to development, the school's trustees identified two important reasons why their philanthropic leadership is key to fund-raising success:

1. *Trustees must set an example.* Early board support provides momentum to both annual and capital campaigns and raises the sights of all subsequent donors. Through their leadership gifts, trustees demonstrate their commitment to the mission and welfare of the school. Their generosity leads others to be generous as well.

2. *Solicitors must make their own gifts first.* Members of the board are key fund-raising solicitors. If they do not make the school a philanthropic priority, how can they ask others to "join me in making a leadership gift to this significant cause"?

As Mary Hundley DeKuyper wrote in the *Trustee Handbook* (NAIS, 1998), "Why should anyone give to the school if the leadership does not give? Trustees need to make significant gifts, according to their abilities to do so, and make them at the beginning of the campaign....The current standard of board participation is 100 percent, and, increasingly, foundations and individuals will give only if it can be demonstrated that all of the trustees have given or pledged."

Donald Green's trustee colleagues defined their fund-raising responsibilities in a manner that was appropriate for and acceptable to all. They agreed upon two principles:

1. Every trustee need not be capable of making a leadership gift, but every trustee must be willing to make early gifts that are generous given his or her family resources. During a capital campaign, every trustee should make the school's needs a personal philanthropic priority.
2. Every trustee need not be capable of making a leadership gift, but those in the community who have major gift potential should be well represented on the board. Because they are trustees, these constituents are more likely to make the major leadership gifts that are essential if the school is to achieve its fund-raising potential.

This second principle reflects an understanding that independent school trustees must be philanthropic pacesetters during a capital campaign. The top campaign gift often comes from a member of the board. And, as a group, trustees typically give at least 30 percent and sometimes as much as 70 percent of the campaign goal.

THE TRUSTEE SOLICITOR

During their development retreat, the trustees discussed another important fund-raising question: Must every trustee solicit gifts?

At many independent schools, the answer is yes. After all, who can better articulate the case for support than a trustee? Who knows more about the annual struggle to pay the faculty a living wage? Who is more committed to offering financial aid to students whose presence enriches the education of all? Who is better informed about the need for a new arts center or gym?

But the trustees at this school preferred a more flexible stance. There were a few members of the board who were happy to put the school's philanthropic needs first but adamant about their refusal to solicit gifts. This led to a third principle of philanthropy for their school:

3. Although the board must have a large corps of willing and able solicitors, every trustee need not agree to solicit gifts before he or she joins the board. However, every trustee must agree to play an active and clearly defined role in the fund-raising process.

THE BOARD'S DEVELOPMENT ROLES

Development is essential to the present and future welfare of all independent schools. Therefore, no trustee can afford to be uninterested in or detached from fund-raising concerns. In addition to making and seeking gifts, every independent school board has seven significant development roles:

1. *Plan the program.* Before a successful fund-raising campaign can begin, a school must have (a) a mission statement, (b) institutional goals and

priorities, (c) a case statement, and (d) a development plan. Trustees, in particular those serving on the strategic planning and development committees, are responsible for making sure that these documents are clear and accurate, regularly reviewed, and frequently updated.

2. *Educate the community.* Trustees are the best spokespersons for the school. It is their task to speak frequently and eloquently about the school's mission, priorities, and goals. Many of these educational opportunities are formal, but just as often they take place on the soccer field or in the car pool line.

3. *Cultivate major prospects.* It is important for each trustee, even those reluctant to solicit, to assume personal responsibility for cultivating several major prospects each year.

4. *Identify potential donors.* When trustees look over the school's entire mailing list at least once a year, they can often identify potential major gift prospects whom they know or know about.

5. *Rate and evaluate potential donors.* Trustees can provide assistance to the development staff by recommending gift levels, appropriate solicitors, or solicitation strategies for prospects whom they know.

6. *Open doors.* A trustee is often the best person to provide an introduction to foundation or corporation representatives and/or to individual potential donors.

7. *Monitor and evaluate success.* The board monitors fund-raising results each month and helps the school head and the development staff evaluate the entire development program each year.

THE KEY ROLES OF THE DEVELOPMENT AND NOMINATING COMMITTEES

At Donald Green's school, the board chair met individually with each trustee to discuss his or her preferred development roles. Those with particular fund-raising interest and expertise were asked to serve on the board's development committee.

The development committee oversees a school's development program; its members assume a leadership role in asking for gifts. The committee works closely with the development director and the school head to approve development program plans and to set goals for annual and capital giving. The committee establishes the school's fund-raising priorities and is responsible for maintaining an active and well-trained volunteer fund-raising corps. It is common for co-opted members (that is, those who are not trustees) to serve on the development committee. Often these co-opted members are subsequently elected to the board.

Figure 3-1

A Development Committee Job Description

A comprehensive job description for the development committee appears in the NAIS publication, Trustee Handbook, *by Mary Hundley DeKuyper. The following is a consolidated version:*

The primary responsibilities of the development committee shall be to advise the board and staff of the school on all matters pertaining to fund raising and to oversee and coordinate the fund-raising efforts of the school. Specific committee responsibilities shall be to:

1. Establish fund-raising goals and organizational structures.

2. Approve the annual fund development plan and inform the board.

3. Monitor annual fund progress.

4. Identify ways in which trustees can be involved in raising funds and match individual board members with the activities that complement his or her skills and interests.

5. Identify and assist with the recruitment of volunteers.

6. Assist with the identification of major donors.

7. Cultivate and solicit major donors, as appropriate.

8. Coordinate plans and activities with the capital campaign committee.

9. Establish and implement a system of recognition for trustees and other volunteers who are active in fund raising.

A sample job description for development committee members appears above in Figure 3-1.

A second board committee whose work has a significant impact on development is the committee on trustees, sometimes called the nominating committee. The committee on trustees selects candidates for the board. The committee functions most effectively when it deliberates throughout the school year and identifies potential trustees well in advance.

To assure that new trustees are willing and able to participate actively in development, the most conscientious committees on trustees pay particular attention to four tasks:

1. *Creating a board profile.* The committee creates a profile of the ideal board based on the school's priorities and needs. Two important categories are always (a) the potential to provide philanthropic leadership and (b) fund-raising interest and skill.

2. *Cultivating potential trustees.* Board candidates are identified well in advance of recruitment and cultivated in a manner (not unlike major donor cultivation) that makes it likely they will accept a future invitation to serve.

Ten Responsibilities of an Independent School Trustee

1. To participate actively and regularly in board meetings and on board committees.

2. To set policy for the school and to take action on budgetary and fiscal proposals.

3. To perpetuate the school's mission and values.

4. To make the school a personal philanthropic priority during the period of trusteeship.

5. To make early contributions to annual and capital fund drives in order to motivate and to raise the sights of subsequent donors.

6. To participate in donor cultivation activities and to solicit contributions with the guidance of the development office.

7. To serve as an advocate of the school in the wider community.

8. To recommend the school, as appropriate, to prospective students, teachers, and other employees.

9. To avoid conflict of interest and the appearance of conflict of interest in all activities on behalf of the school.

10. To participate in an annual trustee self-evaluation and an annual evaluation of the board as a whole.

3. *Recruiting trustees.* Committee members share and discuss a written trustee job description with potential trustees during the recruitment process.
4. *Orienting trustees.* The orientation of new trustees includes an introduction to the school's development challenges as well as a solicitor training session.

Many independent school trustees initially feel uncomfortable asking others for a gift. However, their comfort level often increases dramatically after they attend a solicitor training session and accompany a fellow trustee on a solicitation call.

As one trustee observed, "Soliciting a gift is very much like offering an investment opportunity—only it's easier to sell. What other investment brings such satisfaction to the investor? What other investment makes such a difference in the lives of our youth?"

TRUSTEES AND THE CAPITAL CAMPAIGN

When the chair of Donald Green's board issued invitations to potential new trustees the following spring, Donald and his colleagues were comfortable that the board's fund-raising rules were appropriate and clear.

Several months later, the school launched a capital campaign. In a campaign plan approved by the board, the trustees demonstrated their renewed commitment to development. Unanimously, they pledged:

- To make the capital campaign a personal philanthropic priority.
- To make their pledges at the start of the campaign.
- To look for opportunities to educate others in the school community about the importance of the campaign goals.
- To take on individual cultivation assignments and/or to solicit key prospects.
- To approve the campaign policies, organization, and timetable.
- To evaluate campaign progress each month.

At the start of the campaign, a trustee made a $1-million pledge, a commitment twice the size of any gift the school had received in its 75 years. Within two months, the board had pledged 40 percent of the campaign goal.

The new library, an increased endowment for student financial aid, and a faculty salary stipend plan are the results of this campaign. They are also the legacy of a philanthropically responsible board.

Seven Keys to Board Quality and Effectiveness

1. Diligence of the committee on trustees
2. Balance of strengths and skills among trustees
3. Vigorous cultivation of potential trustees
4. Careful and candid recruitment of new trustees
5. Formal orientation of new trustees
6. Annual board self-evaluation by all trustees
7. Continuing relationship with former trustees

CHAPTER FOUR

MAJOR GIFTS
THE ESSENTIAL ELEMENT
OF FUND-RAISING SUCCESS

People don't give money to an institution they don't feel good about or close to, no matter how worthy it may be. They give money to institutions that reach out and make them feel welcome, important, and needed—because they are.

— **The Successful Capital Campaign**
Edward T. Foote II (CASE, 1986)

First and foremost, development is about people, about building and nurturing relationships with those people whose generosity can empower a school. The best fund-raising programs focus on developing top donors. The most effective fund raisers focus on involving top prospects, on seeking their lifetime loyalty and support.

At every independent school, large or small, urban or rural, old or new, fund-raising success depends upon major gifts. Therefore, major donor research, cultivation, solicitation, and stewardship are the most important professional challenges for directors of development at all schools and at all times.

No matter how excellent a school, how worthy its plans, or how pressing its needs, it will not receive major gifts unless its major prospects are informed and involved, and until they feel needed and committed. Major gifts reflect the depth of the donors' commitment rather than the magnitude of the institution's need.

Therefore, the best major gift fund raisers focus on deepening the donor's commitment to the school. They understand that every major gift prospect is unique. What interests one does not necessarily interest the other. The essence of relationship building is to focus on individuals one by one. The best major gift officers cherish their knowledge of idiosyncrasies that distinguish one prospect from another.

MANY OTHERS HELP

No development officer can build a close relationship with a donor without help. The process almost always includes the school head, trustees, and other volunteers. These people are sometimes referred to as "natural partners" because they have access to the prospective donor and because they are in the best position to determine what kind of approach will be most effective.

In addition, every development staff member plays a role in cultivating major gifts. Today the old distinctions have disappeared; no one individual is only director of annual giving or only director of alumni affairs. Everyone, from the receptionist to the data entry assistant, comes into contact with major donors. Therefore, everyone must know who these donors are as well as how best to cultivate and steward them. Major prospects should be reviewed at development staff meetings, and every staff member should be alert to opportunities to interact with them.

THE ESSENTIAL 10 PERCENT

Because of their importance to the schools, prospects for major and ultimate gifts should occupy a significant amount of every development director's time.

The major gift prospect is an individual whose capacity to give puts him or her in the top 10 percent of the prospect pool. At some schools, this person may have the potential to contribute $10 million; at other schools, a major gift is in the $10,000 range.

This essential 10 percent is likely to give 90 percent of the school's total voluntary support. (In fact, at many schools the top 5 percent gives as much as 95 percent.) Within that group are a few—perhaps only one or two—prospects with the ability to make single gifts that can transform a school; they are prospects for an ultimate gift. Ultimate gifts are usually the largest contributions a donor has ever made and are almost always the largest gifts a school has ever received. Perhaps 1,000 to 10,000 times larger than gifts the donor makes on a regular basis, they come from donors with a deep commitment that's been nurtured over a long period of time.

The donor of an ultimate gift is invariably a previous donor whose giving level has grown over time. One vivid example is Walter H. Annenberg, who in 1993 made a well-publicized $100-million gift to his alma mater, the Peddie School. His support of Peddie began six decades earlier with a small annual gift.

Because of their importance, prospects for major and ultimate gifts—the essential 10 percent—should occupy a significant proportion of every development director's attention and time. This fact is not always well understood by school heads and boards of trustees, notes Virginia D. Howard, former director of development at Potomac School in Virginia and now a fund-raising consultant. As she has said, "My greatest challenge has been helping trustees understand not just their role in development, but also the facts of fund raising. For instance, it is difficult for them to understand that 95 percent of our resources can come from as little as 5 percent of our constituency, and how that translates into staff and trustee allocation of time, programming, and ultimately budget."

RESEARCH AND RATING
Online databases, carefully chosen volunteers, and prospects themselves can be sources of valuable information.

A major gifts program begins with donor research. The purpose is to identify the top 10 percent of the school's prospect pool in terms of capacity to give. Major donor research should be ongoing at all schools, whether or not a capital campaign is about to begin.

Once staff members have identified a major gift prospect, they should undertake further study—using both outside sources and volunteers within the school—to answer three questions:
1. What is this prospect's financial capacity?
2. How strong is the prospect's interest in the school?
3. How philanthropic is the prospect?

For many decades, donor research consisted of studying reference books such as *Who's Who*, *Standard & Poor's*, and *Martindale-Hubbell*. Today, those books and countless other useful databases are online. Computer screening, using a vast variety of sources in the public domain, can identify potential donors far more accurately and quickly than in the past. Some schools do this research in house; others engage a prospect research firm.

Carefully selected volunteers also play an important role in donor research. Their challenge is to rate and screen potential donors whom they know or know about. At donor evaluation sessions, these volunteers assess gift capacity, identify special interests, suggest appropriate gift vehicles, and predict readiness to give. (For sample prospect rating guidelines, see page 39.)

Those who rate and screen should understand two principles:

1. Rating and screening is a confidential process. Its purpose is to make solicitors more sensitive to the prospect's status, feelings, and needs as well as more successful in obtaining generous support.

2. In rating and screening, it is the quality, rather than the quantity, of information that counts. Providing significant insights about only one prospect on a list of 500 may open the door to a major gift.

Sometimes development officers overlook one important information source: the prospects themselves. Personal contact—whether at social events, homecoming, reunions, fund-raising planning sessions, or basketball games—always provides an opportunity to learn more about an individual's philanthropic interests and special concerns.

Development staff should document and save information and advice gleaned during the research process (along with copies of relevant correspondence, clippings, and memos) in confidential electronic and hard-copy files.

The material in those files will help the staff prepare appropriate individual cultivation plans and effective solicitation strategies both now and in the years to come.

DONOR CULTIVATION

Cultivators should say to the prospect, "We'd like to bring you into the inner circle of our school."

Major donor cultivation follows research but precedes the gift request. Cultivation is the process of turning a prospect from an outsider to an insider. An outsider may be aware of a need; an insider is committed to meeting it. An outsider may be informed about a campaign; an insider feels responsible for its success.

Careful, sensitive major donor cultivation is an important prerequisite to solicitation success. Without effective cultivation, the prospect will know less, care less, and give less.

In 2000, Boston College researcher Paul Schervish surveyed 112 families with a net worth of at least $5 million. Ninety-three percent of those interviewed said they would increase their charitable giving if they felt passionate about the cause. The purpose of cultivation is to foster these deep feelings. The process works best when the cultivator listens carefully and tries to involve the major gift prospect in supporting the school's mission in ways that truly excite that passion.

Guidelines for Major Prospect Rating and Screening

Rating

Please use the following numerical rating codes to refer to a prospect's potential for total giving to all charities over a three-year period:

1. $1,000,001 and above
2. $500,001 - $1,000,000
3. $250,001 - $500,000
4. $100,001 - $250,000
5. $50,001 - $100,000
6. $25,000 - $50,000

Please give every prospect you rate a letter code based upon his or her current readiness to make the largest gift of which he or she is capable.

A. Ready to give

B. Needs some cultivation

C. Needs a great deal of additional cultivation

D. Unlikely to give to this campaign

Please add a "star" if it is appropriate to ask the prospect to leave a bequest to the school in his or her will. Please add a "check" if he or she is likely to be interested in another type of planned gift.

Screening

■ Review your list quickly.

■ Evaluate only those whom you know personally. Skip those whom you do not know.

■ Base your fiscal estimate upon what you believe a prospect *can* give to all charities over a three-year period, if sufficiently interested, and not on what you think he or she *will* give.

■ Consider your opinion to be an estimate of potential. We are not depending upon you alone for definitive data. Your evaluation will be considered in light of many other opinions and facts.

Additional Information

In the course of rating, indicate the names of prospects for whom you might be an appropriate solicitor. Indicate as well your suggestions of appropriate solicitors for others.

In addition, when possible, note the following:

■ Components of the campaign that are most likely to interest the prospect.

■ Other family members who might join the prospect in making a group gift.

■ The prospect's potential interest in a named gift.

■ The prospect's other charitable interests.

Major Donor Cultivation

Five Steps for the School:	Six Stages for the Prospect:	Five Qualities of Effective Cultivation:
1. Identify	1. Awareness	1. Candid
2. Inform	2. Knowledge	2. Face-to-Face
3. Interest	3. Interest	3. Frequent
4. Involve	4. Caring	4. Regular
5. Invest	5. Participation	5. Documented
	6. Commitment	

Schools should court their major prospects irrespective of the economy's ups and downs. "For the very high net-worth donor, a major drop in the market does not affect giving decisions. The vast majority of those donors are still working up to their philanthropic potential, and have not even come close to achieving it," noted H. Peter Karoff, chairman of the Philanthropic Initiative, a Boston nonprofit group that counsels donors, in the April 5, 2001, *Chronicle of Philanthropy*.

The best major donor cultivation is candid, one-on-one, and face-to-face.

Here is what the cultivator's words and deeds should suggest to the prospect: "Many people regard you as a potential leader at this school. We feel that if you become knowledgeable and enthusiastic about our goals, we can benefit significantly from your interest, judgment, and support. We'd like to bring you into the inner circle of our school." The cultivator aims to:

- Seek the prospect's friendship and respect.
- Demonstrate to the prospect why he or she should believe in and become personally invested in the school's welfare.
- Persuade the prospect that a project or campaign will have a significant impact and is worthy of particularly generous support.
- Help the prospect understand how important major gifts are to a campaign's success and how personally rewarding major gift philanthropy can be.

Cultivation consists of a series of contacts designed to bring a potential donor closer to the school. These contacts should be regular, frequent, individual, and well planned.

Sometimes the contacts are referred to as "moves," a concept developed in the 1970s by G.T. (Buck) Smith, former president of Chapman College. According to Smith, moves are intended to develop the prospect's awareness of, knowledge of, interest in, involvement with, and eventual commitment to an institution and its mission.

David Dunlop, former director of principal gift fund raising at Cornell

University and one of the country's most-admired fund raisers, said this in the November/December 1990 *CASE Currents*: "If we're not in the hearts and minds of prospective givers every few weeks, other causes they favor will take over more of their attention."

Many schools are conscientious about scheduling contacts with each of their top prospects each month. They nurture relationships with their major prospects at private dinners, during reunion weekends, and at special events. They further strengthen the ties through personal notes and spontaneous telephone calls.

THE RIGHT VOLUNTEERS

Schools must identify volunteers with care, recruit them with vigor, and treat them with respect.

Without the right volunteers, a major gifts program cannot succeed.

Independent schools that achieve their fund-raising potential also invest significant volunteer time in the cultivation process. They form cultivation committees and give individual assignments to their trustees and fund-raising volunteers. And the volunteer is always an essential participant in the major gift request.

Unfortunately, skilled volunteer solicitors are an increasingly scarce and precious resource. Therefore, it is wise to identify them with care, recruit them with vigor, and treat them with respect.

Here are six tips for those who seek a top-notch volunteer solicitor corps.

1. *Recruit the best.* Don't wait for volunteers to volunteer. Go after the ones who will be best and design a job description just for them.
2. *Provide them with facts.* Give a written job description to each volunteer. Include the nature of the task, the time period during which it should be done, and the approximate amount of time it will take.
3. *Respect their time.* Be organized and responsive. Provide agendas for and minutes of meetings. Schedule group meetings only when there is a clear purpose and need. Send discussion materials in advance.
4. *Train even the pros.* Understand that even the most experienced volunteers need training. They may be the top fund raiser at their college or church, but they must learn about the history and needs of your school. They must be well informed about the prospect to be seen, the kind of fund raising you consider appropriate, and the sort of gifts you will accept.
5. *Seek feedback.* Ask volunteers to evaluate their work as well as the nature and timing of services you provide. If they want to meet for breakfast, accommodate them. If they prefer a lunchtime meeting downtown, it's up to you to go.

6. *Thank and thank some more.* Express appreciation for the effort as well as the result. Be certain your volunteers understand that every face-to-face solicitation is by definition a success, regardless of the outcome. A "no" today often becomes a "yes" several years hence.

THE SOLICITATION OF A GIFT
The best solicitors see fund raising as a privilege and a joy.

Planning a major gift solicitation consists of finding the right person to ask the right prospect for the right amount for the right project at the right time.

Major gift solicitation should be done in person by teams of two; at least one solicitor should be the donor's peer. Solicitor No. 1, perhaps the school head, presents the case. Solicitor No. 2, the peer, asks for the gift. For example, he or she may say, "I have just made a six-figure commitment to this campaign. That's a stretch gift for me, a real sacrifice. In fact, it is the largest charitable contribution I have made in my entire life. It demonstrates my belief in the school and in the campaign. I hope you will join me by making a $100,000 pledge at this time."

Who is the best solicitor? Usually, it is someone whom the prospect knows, respects, and admires. Beyond that, the best solicitors are:

- Comfortable asking for gifts.
- Articulate about the joy of giving.
- Deeply committed to the cause.
- Already on board as donors.
- Well briefed about the prospect and the gift to request.
- Fully knowledgeable about the campaign.

Effective solicitors are enthusiastic about the opportunity to bring together a generous donor and a worthy cause. They look upon fund raising as a privilege and a joy. They understand that most prospects view a request for a gift as a compliment. People are often flattered to know that those whom they respect have sufficient faith in their goodness and sensitivity to ask for their support.

GETTING READY TO ASK
A strategy session is vital for making sure both the prospect and the solicitors are ready for the ask.

The donor prospect is ready to be asked. Now it's time for the solicitors to get ready as well.

Each major gift request is a mini campaign unto itself. At a pre-solicitation strategy session, the director of development and the solicitor should ask themselves the following questions:

- How much can this prospect afford to give if our school is his or her major philanthropy over the next three years?
- Is the prospect ready to be asked? Is he or she sufficiently interested and involved in our school and sufficiently invested in the success of our current campaign to make it likely that the gift will match his or her potential? If not, what pre-solicitation cultivation is appropriate?
- Who should be present during the gift solicitation? A spouse? A child? A parent? A financial adviser?
- Who is the right individual to make the request; that is, which solicitor should be responsible for asking for a specific gift?
- When and where should the solicitation take place? In the office or the home? At breakfast or lunch? In the evening?
- Does the prospect have values, traits, or habits that should inform the gift request? For example, does he or she enjoy a leisurely conversation or prefer getting to the point quickly?
- Which aspect of the school's capital agenda would appeal most to the prospect? The new science wing? The new athletic field? An endowed fund?
- Would the prospect be interested in a gift named in honor or in memory of an individual or family member?
- What is the right amount to request at this time?

During the strategy session, the solicitors rehearse by role-playing the conversation they will have. In the process, they seek ways to convey excitement about the opportunity to give; they agree upon the language they will use to invite the donor to give; and they consider questions they may be asked and objections they may need to overcome.

Sometimes it is appropriate to ask a third party to make the appointment for a solicitation visit, to provide access even though he or she will not be present at the meeting. For example, a trustee who knows the donor well, or a beloved teacher, might say, "I would consider it a personal favor if you would see our school head and board chair to discuss a capital campaign gift."

THE VISIT
Every ask requires flexibility, especially if the prospect's first response is no.

Each major gift solicitation is unique, tailor-made for the prospect at hand. However, all skillful solicitations have several common elements as well. The solicitors offer:

- *A positive, enthusiastic approach.* The prospect understands that this is a special moment and a special cause. (That won't happen if a solicitor says, "I'm sorry to intrude on your evening. This will only take a moment of your time.")

- *A personal commitment to the cause.* To illustrate this, the solicitors convey the depth of their own caring and commitment and explain their philanthropic example.

- *A respectful and specific gift request.* For example, a solicitor might say, "In the past, you have invested a total of $100,000 in the needs of our school. Now I am asking you to build on that support by joining me and others who are deeply committed to this campaign. I invite you to consider a $500,000 gift in memory of your father, for whom we would proudly name our new music room."

- *An opportunity for the donor to learn more.* If the solicitors can't answer appropriate questions about the school or the campaign at once, they promise a full and quick response. If the prospect raises concerns, the solicitors address them with sensitivity and care.

- *Flexibility and time to decide.* A leadership gift may take several visits to close. The best solicitors schedule a follow-up meeting, if necessary, during the first encounter.

- *A written proposal to leave behind.* The solicitors may say, "We have summarized our proposal in a letter that you may wish to share with others in your family." If during the visit it becomes apparent that a proposal prepared in advance is inappropriate, the school should send a revised version the following day.

- *Ample thanks.* No matter what transpires, the prospect deserves thanks. He or she has listened to a gift request; he or she has considered a gift. A refusal today may not be a refusal forever. Thanking the prospect for the opportunity to visit and promising to stay in touch makes it much more likely that a gift will be forthcoming at another time.

When a prospect first hears a request for a specific and generous major gift, the first reaction is often no. He or she may say something such as, "Gracious, I can't give $100,000! That is way beyond what I can do!"

At this point, it is up to the solicitor to keep the conversation going. "Would you like to name the science lab in memory of your father?" the solicitor could say. "If so, we will find a way to make it happen." Perhaps the donor will decide to pledge now but to make no payments for a few years, or combine outright and deferred support, or consider a joint gift with a sibling.

For the solicitor, the key is to remain flexible, to offer alternatives, and to ask questions. Very often, prospective donors move from "no" to "yes" during this process.

For first-time solicitors as well as for long-time pros, here's a solicitation checklist:

A Solicitor's Checklist

The Homework
☐ Know the case for support.
☐ Know your prospect.
☐ Make your own pledge first.

The Preparation
☐ Telephone for an appointment at a time and place convenient for the prospect.
☐ Rehearse the conversation you will have. Decide which solicitor will present the case, which will ask for the gift, etc.

The Visit
☐ *The introduction.* Thank the prospect for the opportunity to visit and to discuss a matter critical to the future of the school.
☐ *The school update.* Discuss the special merits and current strengths and accomplishments of the school.
☐ *The case.* Present the case for support.
☐ *The fund-raising update.* Discuss fund-raising progress to date and the importance of leadership support.
☐ *The gift request.* Ask for a specific commitment, if possible for a purpose that will have special appeal.
☐ *The close.* Offer to return with more information or for a further discussion after the donor has thought about a gift. If the prospect does not make a commitment, set a date for a follow-up visit or call. Leave or promise to send a written version of your gift request.

The Follow-up
☐ Send a letter of thanks.
☐ Send a solicitor report form to the development office.

Too often, solicitors overlook the follow-up. Reports (in writing, by-email, or by phone) about a major gift solicitation are invaluable. They assure proper staff follow-up. They inform future gift requests. They help the school raise funds in a manner that gives the donor's feelings and preferences their proper weight. (For a sample report format, see page 47.)

STEWARDSHIP

Each top prospect is a treasure who should be treated with sensitivity and care before, during, and after the gift request.

Stewardship is cultivation after the gift. It is the process of maintaining and nurturing a donor's relationship to the school, of making him or her feel good about the gift.

Basic to good gift stewardship are (1) prompt, accurate, and warm thanks and (2) the assurance—repeated over and over again—that the gift is having a significant impact on the school and being used as the donor requested.

Acknowledgment of a very large gift should reflect its significance to the school. A telephone call from the school head or a hand-delivered letter from the campaign chair should come on the day on which the gift is received. Thereafter, others should send personal and meaningful expressions of sincere gratitude.

Furthermore, leadership gift acknowledgement should never end. The donor who provides the naming gift for an arts center should be invited not only to the dedication but also to plays and musicals in future years. The donor whose gift was used to name the gym should be an honored guest at major sports events many years hence.

What if the school has not been a good steward? How should staff or volunteers approach a benefactor long ignored? Most experienced fund raisers agree that it's never too late for stewardship to begin. A dinner to honor a leadership donor a decade after his or her gift can be a first step to reconnecting a major prospect with the school.

Compared to colleges and universities, the number of major gift prospects at most independent schools is small. Therefore, each top prospect is a treasure who should be treated with sensitivity and care before, during, and after the gift request. Major gift prospects—that essential 10 percent—should know that they are important and needed—because they are!

THE REYNOLDS SCHOOL
MAJOR GIFT SOLICITOR'S REPORT

(Anyone using this report may send it by e-mail, U.S. mail, or by phone. It may even be dictated into the development director's voicemail. Using one of these methods, a solicitor should send the report very soon— always within a week after the solicitation visit.)

Date _____

Solicitor's name _____

Date of visit _____

Name of prospect _____

Summary of visit (include all relevant financial, biographical, and school-related data)

_____

_____

_____

_____

_____

Did the prospective donor make a commitment?   Yes   No

If so, what amount? _____

Did he or she sign a letter of intent?   Yes   No

Does the prospective donor need additional information from the development office?   Yes   No

If so, specify (fiscal facts, planned gift information, etc.)

_____

_____

CHAPTER FIVE

THE SCHOOL HEAD'S ROLE IN DEVELOPMENT
Near the Top of Denise Harris's List

"You'll be a teacher's teacher, a CEO, a financial planner, a personnel evaluator, a family counselor, a child psychologist, a crisis manager, a curriculum designer, a plant supervisor, and a pastor as well. But if you're going to be a successful school head in today's world, you must be an effective, enthusiastic fund raiser, too. Your development duties must always be near the top of your list."

D enise Harris, the new head at an independent school, listens carefully as the board chair uses the words above to characterize her challenge.

Denise is not surprised; she knows that a school head must think about development every day. If the institution is to thrive, large sums must be raised. And if large sums are to be raised, the head must be intimately involved in fund raising.

In a very real sense, every head who runs a strong school is making a major contribution to its development success. Fund-raising efforts flourish at schools that are calm and well led, where the education is exciting and the atmosphere is joyful.

However, in addition, a school head has specific and time-consuming development duties. Committing 20 percent of their time to fund raising is common for school heads. However, some devote 40 to 50 percent of their time, particularly during a capital campaign.

When wearing the development hat, the school head is:

- The chief communicator of the school's vision, mission, and goals.
- The leader of internal and external development teams.
- The cultivator of major gift prospects.
- The solicitor of leadership gifts.
- The evaluator of the development program and the supervisor of its chief.

COMMUNICATION: SETTING THE STAGE
It's all about education.

Donors give generously to schools they understand, appreciate, and admire. As chief communicator, the school head sets the stage for fund-raising success. He or she inspires commitment to the school's mission and generates enthusiasm for its current goals.

Whenever a school head talks or writes about the school, he or she is helping to raise funds. More than anyone else, the head has the golden opportunity to convey the institution's spirit, uplift and unify its community, and personify its values.

Every school head has the responsibility to educate and to excite trustees, faculty, staff, students, parents, alumni, parents of alumni, grandparents, and friends. Board committee meetings, back-to-school nights, alumni reunions, grandparent days, faculty meetings, athletic events, school plays, student assemblies—these and countless other events provide opportunities to inform those close to the school. Columns in school magazines, in newsletters, on Web sites, and in annual reports help the head reach the community at large.

BUILDING THE INTERNAL TEAM
Too often, development is poorly understood within the school.

At her school, Denise Harris knows that before she can raise significant sums, she must build a strong fund-raising team.

Her first challenge is to educate members of the faculty and administration about the positive impact generous voluntary support has on them all. She has found that the field of development and the work of the development office are poorly understood within the school. She wants her teachers and staff to understand and to appreciate the work of her fine development professionals She also plans to inform the faculty and staff about the time-consuming nature and importance of her own development role.

Furthermore, she expects the school's top administrators to be supportive members of the development team and to work with the development director in an atmosphere of confidence and trust. If this group works together well:

- The business manager will contact the director of development before calling a top campaign prospect to complain about an overdue tuition bill.
- The admissions director will consult the development director about the most sensitive way to reject the child of an important alumna.
- The college guidance director will understand that the development director wants to congratulate a major donor about his child's early admission to college.
- The upper school principal will alert the development director when the capital campaign chair's child fails a course.

INSPIRING THE EXTERNAL TEAM
If top volunteers fail to take their roles seriously, even the best-planned campaign will flounder.

Equally important is the external development team of fund-raising leaders and volunteers. Team building begins with the board of trustees. Denise knows that if the board is not committed to development, and if its members don't take their roles as fund raisers and philanthropists seriously, even the best-planned fund-raising campaign will flounder. Therefore, she has planned a discussion and reaffirmation of the board's development role at its fall retreat.

Denise also knows that, to provide fund-raising leadership for trustees and volunteers, she must work closely and collaboratively with the board chair and the development director. The head, board chair, and development director must set an example of collegiality, respect, and trust if they wish to attract high-caliber volunteers.

Finally, it is the head's particular responsibility to convey deep gratitude to those top volunteers who give generously of their talent and time. Volunteers whose service is acknowledged and appreciated throughout a school community are invariably more invested in its success, more effective in marketing its goals, and more generous in supporting its campaigns.

ESTABLISHING RAPPORT WITH PROSPECTS
Many school heads look upon cultivation as a respite.

One of the most important development jobs of any school head is to build a personal relationship with those who can do the most for the school—the 10 percent of the constituency who will provide 90 to 95 percent of the voluntary support. If the prospect is a trustee or current parent, it is easier to establish rapport in the normal course of events. It is more of a challenge when the prospect is an alumnus who lives far away or a grandparent who seldom comes to town.

Sometimes the head can meet a top prospect at a campus lunch for two, but often the lunch is many miles away. For every major prospect whom a head sees on the sidelines at the weekly varsity soccer game, there's another who must be visited in a distant state.

However, Denise knows that travel for development purposes is time well spent because major donor cultivation has everything to do with the size of the eventual gift. Furthermore, it's a pleasant task. Many school heads see cultivation as a respite, an opportunity to spread pride and joy. In addition, the school head who gets to know his or her major prospects well often makes lifetime friends. What begins as donor cultivation ends as a personal bond.

THE SCHOOL HEAD AS SOLICITOR
Like all other solicitors, the school head must learn how to strategize and how to solicit a major gift. Five solicitation principles are key.

1. The top gift must come first.
It's tempting for a head to go first to someone easy to approach. But it's good fund-raising practice to solicit the top prospect first so that his or her commitment can raise the sights of all donors to come.

2. Every visit is a success.
Every personal appeal a school head makes is worthwhile, even if the answer is no. The prospect knows and remembers that the head came to visit. Especially if the head makes an effort to sustain the relationship, interest in and loyalty to the school are likely to grow.

3. Always take a peer.
The best major gift solicitation is done by teams. The head speaks eloquently for and about the school. The peer then says, "Now, my friend, may I invite you to join me in making a six-figure gift?"

4. Beware the manipulative gift.
A school head must never permit a donor to alter school policy with a generous gift. Many heads have reluctantly turned down large sums in order to remain true to the school's vision and mission. No gift should come with unwanted strings attached.

5. Thank and thank some more.
The best fund-raising heads take the time to express appreciation over and over

again. A leadership gift always merits a phone call, then a letter, and—whenever possible—a handshake as well.

FUND RAISING FROM THE HEAD'S POINT OF VIEW

It's always a pleasure to bring together a generous prospect and a worthy cause.

Just as solicitation presents special challenges for the head, the entire development program also looks different from the top. As Denise Harris considers her development agenda, she plans to pay particular attention to:

A manageable menu.

All school heads need a few well-defined development objectives for each school year. A first year is not the best time to redesign the entire

Staffing for Success

Fund-raising success depends upon carefully made plans carried out by competent personnel.

Although the development director oversees the formulation of these plans, it is up to the school head to assure that the planning process takes place and that a clear, well-prioritized plan is established and evaluated each year.

The head is also responsible for recruiting a high-caliber professional to lead the development staff. Even the smallest or newest school should have at least one development officer who is responsible for organizing the program and providing fund-raising expertise. A school without a development professional may raise increasing amounts of money each year. However, it cannot expect to fulfill its true fund-raising potential in the present or to ensure significant growth in voluntary support in the years to come.

It is no accident that schools with the highest levels of voluntary support also have the largest development staffs. A day school with 1,000 students and a full-scale development program often has an advancement staff (professional and support) of six to 10. A day school with 500 students may have a development office of five or six. Other key factors that determine staff size are the age of the school and the size and location of the alumni corps. In addition to managing fund-raising appeals, development professionals are usually responsible for alumni relations, publications, special events, and public relations.

Few school heads can afford the staffs of more than 30 that some of the country's oldest New England boarding schools have assembled to reach their far-flung and generous alumni corps. On the other hand, it is never cost-effective for a school head to run a development program alone.

program. Instead, a new head might choose three specific goals, such as getting to know five top prospects, reviewing publications, and studying the development office's computer needs. It's never wise to change too much too soon.

The million-dollar gift.

No matter how small, young, or rural a school is, somewhere in the community is a prospect with the capacity to make a million-dollar gift. Perhaps the prospect is an alumnus who hasn't visited his alma mater in a decade, or a grandmother who has been on campus only once. Every head should find that prospect and start a cultivation process even though it may be years before it's time to solicit a major gift.

The appropriateness test.

The school head's instincts count. If a fund-raising formula, program, or technique seems inappropriate given the school's culture, climate, or history, it's up to the head to say no—or at least "not yet."

The joy of success.

It's always a pleasure to bring together a generous prospect and a worthy cause. It's very satisfying to see a concrete result, such as a new arts center, library, or gym. This is particularly true for a school head because raising money presents a challenge so different from other tasks. Teaching and learning are complex processes best evaluated over time. In contrast, a campaign is simple and clear: There is a goal, a timetable, and, most often, 100 percent success.

CHAPTER SIX

CATCHING THE DONOR'S EYE
BEGIN WITH THE ANNUAL GIFT

Virtually anyone can become a philanthropist—a recognized one—just by making a modest annual gift to a worthy organization.... By asking for a small annual gift, and getting it, an organization moves up tremendously in the donor's scheme of things. It has an easier claim to the donor's attention and interest. And, of course, this is the route to the truly big donation: the capital or deferred gift.

— The FRI Annual Giving Book
M. Jane Williams (Fund-Raising Institute, 1981)

Philanthropy begins with the annual gift. It is the foundation upon which capital giving and planned giving are built. It is the program through which top prospects and volunteers emerge. It is the means by which a school continuously educates the community about its present plans and future goals. It is an important vehicle for stewardship.

Annual gifts produce current operating revenue; they are spent in the year received or, in the case of a few schools, in the subsequent year. Most often, annual gifts are unrestricted. However, in some cases, the donor asks that a gift be used for a particular purpose. If such restricted gifts are to be counted in the annual fund, they must be earmarked for a program funded by the operating budget and spent in their entirety in the current (or following) school year.

All of this is in contrast to capital gifts, which underwrite new or improved facilities (not included in the annual operating budget) or increase the school's endowment fund. Gifts for endowment go into the school's savings to be held and invested in perpetuity; only a portion of the income they produce is spent.

Broad participation in annual giving is vitally important. Even small gifts boost the percentage, or rate, of participation. Foundations that support independent schools often take into account the parent and alumni participation rate as they decide whether to lend their own support. Percentages also affect major donors who like to know that their commitment is broadly shared.

Annual giving programs should produce increased dollar amounts and increased percentages of operating revenue each year. However, some annual drives plod along year after year without real growth. They may provide more money, but as a percentage of the budget, they lose ground.

Most often, such programs have two flaws: They are too impersonal, and they treat prospects alike when, in fact, these prospects have very different relationships with the school. The hallmark of the generic approach is a standard appeal letter that begins, "Dear Friend," and goes out to the entire mailing list.

In contrast, annual giving programs that thrive use the opposite approach.

- *They segment prospects into many different groups.* Each group receives separate fund-raising initiatives geared to gift potential, giving history, constituency (parent, grandparent, etc.), or the special purpose of the request.
- *They rely upon a personal appeal.* The solicitation—be it in person, on the phone, or by mail—is from a peer whom the prospect knows and respects.

SETTING GOALS
Mature annual giving may provide an average of 8 to 10 percent of annual operating revenue.

Every school should have an annual giving plan that covers four aspects of the drive: the overall objectives, the strategy for soliciting each group, the timetable for solicitation, and the fiscal goals. Of these tasks, goal setting is invariably the most challenging.

Most schools rely upon voluntary support to cover an operating shortfall. Therefore, schools should establish their annual giving goals when they set their budget. The budgeted goal should be low enough to appear achievable yet high enough to challenge the staff and volunteers.

Mature annual giving programs contribute an average of 8 to 10 percent of annual operating revenue each year. However, among independent schools, the range is wide. At some schools, particularly well-established boarding schools, annual giving provides as much as 12 to 15 percent of total income. At other schools, it provides as little as 4 percent.

Sometimes, trustees and business managers lobby for substantial one-year increases in annual giving goals. However, experienced fund raisers know that they should project steady annual increases rather than a giant gain in any one year. In addition, boards should realize that they are unlikely to raise major sums without spending money to do so. Typically schools spend 12 to 15 cents on fund raising for every annual giving dollar raised.

Annual giving goals should be calculated both as a dollar amount and as a percentage of the school's total operating income. Using that method, it becomes clear when a program that raises an increased amount of money is actually producing a smaller percentage of total income each year. (See "Is the Annual Fund Really Growing?" on page 66.)

Once a school has set an overall goal, the staff should establish sub-goals for each constituency group. At most schools, the total of these constituency goals exceeds the overall goal in order to accommodate unpredictable variations from year to year.

DIVIDE AND CATEGORIZE

Potential donors are not the same. Annual giving appeals shouldn't be, either.

Usually a school will ask all constituents—alumni, parents, parents of alumni, grandparents, and friends—for an annual gift. The staff sends at least one appeal letter to even the most unlikely prospects, including alumni who graduated many years ago, live far away, and have never made a gift.

However, it is never good fund-raising practice to approach all constituents in the same way or to ask them all for the same amount. Potential donors are not the same; understanding and responding to their many differences is a prerequisite to fund-raising success.

Here, for example, are five categories to take into account in designing an annual giving drive.

1. Gift potential.

Those who have the potential to make the largest gifts should be approached first, in person, with a request for a generous amount. Their early support will provide momentum for the drive, and their generosity will raise subsequent donors' sights.

2. Giving history.

The school should make an effort to acknowledge and praise consistent support over many years and increased gift levels each year. The staff should plan special approaches for donors who gave last year but not this year (LYBUNTS) and donors who gave at some time in the past but not this year (SYBUNTS). In requesting gifts from those who have provided past support, the staff should always begin with "thank you" before proceeding to "please."

3. Relationship to the school.

Different constituent groups—alumni, parents, parents of alumni, grandparents—think about their annual support in different ways. Parents, for example, may consider their annual gifts an investment in the school today. They like to know how their support will benefit their own children this year or next. On the other hand, alumni are likely to think of annual giving as an opportunity to express appreciation for the experiences they had in the past and as a way to provide today's students with the same high-quality education.

The possibilities for segmentation are endless. Some schools appeal separately to families with multi-generational ties. Others design separate campaigns for regional or professional groups.

A prospect's relationship to the school can also determine the proper form of a gift request. Grandparent phonathons don't work as well as personal handwritten letters from a peer. Young alumni may respond best to an e-mail or phone call from a classmate.

4. This particular year.

The moment in time also affects the nature of the appeal. To establish a pattern of annual giving, it's important to give alumni in their first or second postgraduate years special attention. Their letters and calls should emphasize the importance of even very small gifts because foundations look at alumni participation rates when they evaluate grant requests.

The school should encourage alumni celebrating important five-year reunions (5th, 10th, 15th, etc.) to acknowledge those milestones with increased levels of support. For the 25th and 50th reunions, in particular, schools often ask alumni to make particularly generous gifts to meet a special institutional need.

In a similar way, schools ask parents of seniors for larger gifts at graduation and when their children celebrate important reunion years.

5. Purpose of the gift request.

Often, annual giving initiatives are designed to achieve an ancillary or special purpose. A solicitor may visit a non-donor in person as part of a major gift cultivation plan. An annual giving caller may converse with a major prospect at greater length to assess his or her commitment to the school. The school may recruit a potential capital campaign solicitor or potential trustee to chair the annual giving drive in order to evaluate leadership skills and foster loyalty.

Establishing Timetables

The annual giving timetable should encompass every season of the year.

Summer is the time to get ready—to plan the campaign, to write the case, to compose cover letters, to print letterhead and pledge cards.

The fall months, September through December, are key solicitation times. At least one solicitation (in person, by phone, or mail, or some combination thereof) should reach each potential donor before the end of the calendar year. Most schools also schedule a December reminder, since many donors make decisions about their charitable giving at year-end.

Winter and early spring are times to pay special attention to habitual donors who have not yet made their gifts, to new parents who should be encouraged to establish a pattern of annual giving, and to groups that have been targeted for special attention during the current campaign.

Spring is also the time to think ahead to the upcoming school year and to recruit volunteers, establish new strategies, and confirm goals.

At the end of the school's fiscal year comes an especially important event on the annual giving calendar: the evaluation of the previous year's program and results. Asking staff, administration, development committee, and fund-raising volunteers to assess progress is essential to every professional drive. Without evaluation, there is little likelihood that the program will improve from year to year.

Every school should experiment with at least one new form of constituency segmentation each year. Innovation and change not only improve fund-raising results; they also make a recurring program far more interesting and stimulating for the staff and volunteers.

PREPARING THE CASE FOR SUPPORT: EIGHT KEY QUESTIONS

You've been asked to draft your school's annual giving case for support. Perhaps it's a simple brochure to send with an appropriate letter or to be presented in person during a solicitation call. As you write, there are eight key questions you should ask yourself:

1. Does the case sell the school?

What makes the school unique? Why is it worthy of support? What were its special strengths and successes in recent years? The purpose of a fund-raising appeal is to excite potential donors about the school. That always comes first!

2. Does the case document the need?

Why does the school need annual support this year? Even though you're seeking unrestricted gifts, it's important to explain how they will help. Will they improve the academic program or meet another specific need? How can you document the need from a fiscal point of view? Potential donors are keenly interested in specific details about the ways in which their investments will improve the school.

3. Does the case create a sense of urgency?

Why give by June 15? That is the school's cutoff for an annual gift, but why should it matter to a donor? It is always a challenge to convince annual fund donors that their support within a specific time frame is important. You can create a sense of urgency by focusing on the more immediate tax benefits of a gift made in December rather than the following year. You can also do this through the "printer's proof," a list of donors you send out in the late spring that acknowledges gifts already received and reminds LYBUNTS and non-donors that the cutoff for this year's annual fund donor list is near.

4. Does the case make it clear that every gift counts?

Many an annual fund prospect asks, "If the school's budget is $15 million, why does my $100 gift count?" You can answer this in two ways:

Emphasize the fact that percentages are important. Foundations that support independent schools almost always inquire about the percentage of parent and alumni annual support as they make their grant decisions.

Provide examples of tangible ways in which modest gifts can help. A $100 gift, for example, may buy a new set of teaching materials or provide gym uniforms for financial-aid students.

5. Does the case convey gratitude for support?

The case should convey the school's deep appreciation for those who give generously year after year. Express thanks not only in the text but also in personal letters of appeal, during solicitation calls, by acknowledging donors in annual reports, through gift clubs, and at special events.

6. Does the case avoid the implication that the gift requested is a debt?

An annual gift is not an obligation; it's voluntary support. As Harold J. Seymour wrote in *Designs for Fund-Raising* (Taft Group, 1999), "Uncle Sam can talk about what you owe him and get his money. But voluntary causes should know by this time that it is a sterile gambit indeed to tell prospective donors that they owe the institution something because service to them was rendered at less than cost."

Independent schools sometimes overemphasize the fact that tuition does not cover the full cost of educating a student, thereby creating an implication of debt. It's far more effective to stress the school's need for support in order to provide an excellent education and its wish to hold down tuition increases in order to provide greater access for those who cannot afford the cost.

7. Does the case put the cause before the goal?

Fiscal goals do many important things. They keep the staff on its toes; they motivate fund-raising volunteers; they provide measures of success; they are an essential budget-planning tool. But fiscal goals rarely motivate donors to give.

All annual giving professionals should remember that the fiscal goal is the school's—not the donor's. The case for support should seek a gift to achieve an institutional dream or to meet a pressing and demonstrable need. It should not seek a gift primarily to achieve a fiscal goal.

8. Finally, does the case convey a consistent marketing message to prospects every year?

Sometimes, when the school leaves the design and tone of an annual giving case to volunteer leaders who rotate annually, the message may change too much from year to year. This can become confusing for the donor. A far better approach is to give annual giving a standard look, perhaps using the same size brochure, the same colors or logo, or the same typeface each year, so the donor will recognize it.

THE VOLUNTEER ROLE

The volunteer makes possible a broad-based, peer-to-peer, personal approach that increases the likelihood of a generous gift.

Annual giving, like all fund raising, depends upon volunteers.

There's very little that annual giving volunteers can't do. They can help in the office by answering the phone, stuffing envelopes, and writing thank-you notes. They can host meetings to train solicitors and parties to celebrate success. They can take top prospects to lunch for a cultivation visit or gift request. They can open their own offices for phonathons and, sometimes, even underwrite the cost of the calls.

The Family of Funds

An annual giving approach that has become newly popular is the family of funds. Schools are using this marketing tool to let donors choose to allocate their gifts to one or more broad gift opportunities—such as arts, athletics, financial aid, faculty, campus maintenance, or technology. The funds contributed provide operating budget relief only, not additional restricted funds for a particular area of school life. An accompanying disclaimer explains that the board of trustees retains the discretion to use these annual giving proceeds to support the school's general operations should contributions for a particular purpose exceed the expenditure limits provided in that year's operating budget.

The family-of-funds approach is a marketing device only; it does not change the board-designated allocation of funds. However, many annual giving directors have found that offering donors the opportunity to direct their gifts fosters more generous support and helps the school provide a consistent message each year.

Although many development officers help to solicit annual gifts, it is the volunteer who makes possible a broad-based, peer-to-peer personal approach. And the more personal the appeal, the greater the likelihood of a generous gift. Given the increasing number of causes seeking philanthropic support, schools that can solicit the top 10 percent of their prospect pool face-to-face are far more likely to achieve ambitious goals. (For prospects whom volunteers cannot see in person, it's effective to contact them by e-mail or telephone and to follow up with a note re-emphasizing the need and acknowledging any commitment the prospects made.)

Many schools conduct up-front phonathons in October or early November, using trustees and other key volunteers as callers. The phone call is more personal than the mailed piece and more likely to secure the larger gifts on which schools must increasingly depend to attain higher annual fund goals. Other schools first send a direct mail piece that tells addressees to expect a call and asks them to think about a leadership-level commitment.

Alumni often look forward to phonathons as a chance to reconnect with classmates. Nevertheless, the combination of caller ID, answering machines, and increasing numbers of telephone solicitations may mean that the phonathon has a limited future. Some schools have already substituted audio- or videotape solicitations for the phonathon. Many others are depending more on e-mail than on the telephone.

Whatever the solicitation timetable, sequence, or vehicle, in this computer age it is a rare school that can't produce a personal approach to every donor capable of or likely to offer generous annual support.

The most effective volunteer organizations have separate annual giving chairs and committees for leadership gifts and for each constituency group—alumni, parents, parents of alumni, grandparents, and friends. As important as it is to recruit new volunteers each year, it's equally wise to re-enlist top-notch solicitors. After all, who is more likely to give than a previous committee member who has helped to solicit gifts?

It is also important to provide chairs and committee members with written descriptions of their volunteer jobs. For example, one school told the annual giving co-chairs when they were recruited that they would be asked to:

- Review solicitation materials and share reactions with the development staff.
- Help to recruit and to motivate annual giving committee members.
- Preside at annual giving committee meetings and speak publicly about the importance of annual giving to the school's welfare.
- Help to recognize and to thank donors and volunteers.
- Make an early and generous gift that reflects the priority they assign to the campaign and that will serve as an example for others.

MATCHING TECHNIQUES AND SCHOOLS

For every annual giving objective, there's an appropriate fund-raising technique. The challenge for each school is to identify the techniques that work best and are most appropriate within its particular milieu. The following initiatives work well at many schools.

Pace-setting gifts

Throughout the nonprofit world, fewer donors are giving a larger percentage of the total raised. Annual giving results reflect this trend. The top gifts have greater importance each year. To attract pace-setting gifts, annual gift fund raisers often:

- Ask several top prospects to offer a challenge to other major gift prospects or perhaps to the board of trustees.
- Solicit top prospects early with specific gift requests, explaining that their generosity will not only help the school but also inspire subsequent donors to give more.
- Increase the gift level required for the top gift club and acknowledge top donors in an annual report.

■ Offer donors who make the largest gifts the opportunity to attend an appealing special event and send them several "special friend" letters during the school year.

Habitual gifts

Annual giving also depends upon donors who remember the school each year. Schools encourage habitual giving in several ways:

■ Maintain predictable solicitation timetables each year.

■ Establish gift clubs or provide special recognition opportunities for donors whose support has been uninterrupted for five, 10, or 20 years.

■ Acknowledge the total amount given and the number of uninterrupted years of annual support in individual letters of appeal.

Larger gifts

If annual giving totals are to grow, a group of donors must increase their gifts each year. To attract increased gifts, many schools:

■ Respectfully request specific increases in personal letters of appeal.

■ Seek a foundation challenge to be matched by donors who increase their annual gifts.

■ Establish a gift club for those who increase their gifts by a set percentage—for example, 20 percent each year.

First gifts

Every successful drive must attract new donors each year. To do so, schools often:

■ Ask a foundation or individual to match the total that first-time donors contribute to the drive.

■ Give special attention to those who have never made a gift or whose last gift was many years ago. Some schools employ telemarketing firms to approach these groups; the gifts received more than cover the cost of the effort. However, when a school uses a telemarketing firm, the staff should carefully monitor the process and approve the nature, tone, content, timing, and all other aspects of the solicitation delivered on its behalf.

■ Make it easier to give by offering donors the opportunity to charge a gift to a credit card. There are many advantages to this approach, as Virginia D. Howard explains in *A Development Handbook: Promoting Philanthropy at Independent Schools* (CASE, 1992): "Most banks offer schools a reduced rate on credit card financing of gifts, and this can be very convenient for donors. From the school's perspective, the gift is made as soon as the charge is

THE REYNOLDS SCHOOL
Annual Fund Tracking and Evaluation Chart

		Total $ Raised	Total # of Gifts	# of First Gifts	# of LYBUNTS	Highest Gift	Lowest Gift	Average Gift
Parents	Year 1							
	Year 2							
Alumni	Year 1							
	Year 2							
Grandparents	Year 1							
	Year 2							
Alum. Parents	Year 1							
	Year 2							
Friends	Year 1							
	Year 2							
Foundations	Year 1							
	Year 2							
Corp. Matches	Year 1							
	Year 2							

THE REYNOLDS SCHOOL

Is the Annual Fund Really Growing?

Annual Giving Expressed as a Percentage of Operating Budget

Year	Annual Giving	Budget Actual	Percentage of Budget
Year 1	$464,890	$5,405,700	8.6
Year 2	$450,789	$5,706,200	7.9
Year 3	$400,995	$5,985,000	6.7
Year 4	$414,080	$6,470,000	6.4
Year 5	$420,080	$7,120,000	5.9
Year 6	$450,555	$7,768,204	5.8
Year 7	$502,842	$8,243,308	6.1
Year 8	$487,455	$8,862,815	5.5
Year 9	$528,128	$9,265,400	5.7

cleared, and money saved through not mailing pledge reminders can cover fees charged by the bank."

As all good fund raisers know, the work does not end when the gift is received. Accurate record keeping, prompt acknowledgment, and sincere thanks are essential elements of annual giving success. Donors of small sums who believe that the school warmly appreciates them will feel good about their gifts and care more about the cause. In this way, annual giving can foster a philanthropic spirit that will benefit the school in the years to come.

CHAPTER SEVEN

GET READY, GET SET, GO

KEY ELEMENTS OF A CAPITAL CAMPAIGN

Sell the opportunities and not the deficiencies, never forgetting that money flows to promising programs and not to needy institutions.

— Designs for Fund-Raising
Harold J. Seymour (Taft Group, 1999)

All successful capital campaigns are different, even those at the same school. Between campaigns, both a school and its priorities change. Voluntary support moves to a higher plateau. New prospects are found and new leadership emerges.

Therefore, a campaign today should be more sophisticated and comprehensive than the same school's campaign a decade ago. Fund-raising progress during the intervening years should be reflected in a higher goal and a larger, more committed volunteer corps.

At the same time, all successful capital campaigns are similar. They are carefully planned well in advance and managed by a competent staff. The planning includes not only a clear analysis of priority capital needs (often documented in a strategic institutional plan) but also a careful evaluation of leadership gift potential throughout all constituencies. Successful capital campaigns are led by an involved school head and a committed board, and they are empowered by an articulate, well-respected, and generous solicitor corps.

Are We Ready?

Some schools begin campaigns too soon. They test campaign readiness with a feasibility study before they've done their homework. They set their sights on an unrealistic goal even though their development director doubts it can be achieved. In short, they base their plans upon capital needs alone, not on fund-raising progress and potential as well.

Campaigns that begin too soon frequently fail. Feasibility studies undertaken prematurely are a waste of school money and staff time. It always pays to wait, to take time to get ready. The board and administration should be able to answer yes to the following 11 questions before beginning a capital campaign.

1. Do you have a clear mission statement and a strategic plan that identifies specific goals for the next five years?

2. Do you have a written case for support that identifies a valid and urgent need and that will excite potential donors and inspire generous support?

3. Does your board feel responsible for the success of the drive?

4. Do you have trustees who are willing and able to solicit leadership gifts?

5. Have you researched and rated your entire donor pool?

6. Have you cultivated those who are most capable of major support?

7. Do you have a fund-raising track record with a corps of constituents who have made habitual gifts to your school?

8. Can you identify strong potential campaign leaders and a sufficiently large corps of potential campaign volunteers?

9. Is your school head willing to spend his or her time articulating the challenge, cultivating prospects, and soliciting gifts?

10. Can your development office staff service a campaign effectively and professionally? Are your development office systems adequate and your gift policies clear?

11. Do your constituents think highly of your school? In particular, have any recent crises or controversies been solved?

Three documents should undergird every independent school capital campaign: a case statement, a feasibility study, and a campaign plan. Together these documents provide a demonstration of need; an analysis of potential; and a compilation of campaign policies, timetables, and plans. Because the school typically completes the case statement, feasibility study, and campaign plan before seeking a single gift, people sometimes say that the most important work of a capital campaign takes place before it actually begins.

THE CASE FOR SUPPORT

A well-written case statement appeals to both hearts and minds.

A case statement describes, justifies, and documents the school's capital needs within the context of its past successes and future goals. The case statement is an investment prospectus. Like all sales documents, it should be brief, simple, and clear. It should convey a sense of optimism about the school and reinforce feelings of loyalty and commitment on the part of those who are capable of major support.

As Harold J. Seymour wrote in *Designs for Fund-Raising* (Taft Group, 1999), the case should "aim high, provide perspective, arouse a sense of history and continuity, convey a feeling of importance, relevance, and urgency, and have whatever stuff is needed to warm the heart and stir the mind."

In *Fund Raising and the Nonprofit Board* (National Center for Nonprofit Boards, 1988), Fisher Howe describes the essence of a case statement in these words: "The case sets out in compelling terms the reasons for making a supportive contribution. It interprets and explains the mission for prospective donors, looking at the organization from the supporters' point of view."

The case should answer all relevant questions—who, what, why, when, and how—about the institutional needs to be met and the campaign specifically designed to meet these needs. A typical case statement has these eight components:

1. Summary
2. The school's mission
3. The current needs
4. A campaign to meet these needs
5. The number and level of gifts required
6. Ways to give
7. Recognition opportunities
8. Campaign leaders

THE FEASIBILITY STUDY

Feasibility studies are a predictor of and guide to campaign success.

The case statement describes the needs a campaign will meet. The feasibility study assesses the school's readiness and ability to meet these needs. Simply put, it is a pre-campaign market survey.

The market is the school's community of potential major donors and top volunteers, those who will make the capital campaign a success. The survey determines how they feel about the school and the fund drive. It assesses their level of knowledge, personal involvement, and philanthropic commitment. It is a predictor of and guide to campaign success.

A feasibility study focuses on people (both donors and volunteers) and gifts (both the levels and numbers needed) in order to make recommendations about the total amount of money the school can raise and the length of time it will take to reach the goal. (See a sample outline on page 80.)

Good feasibility studies have significant value. In addition to assessing campaign readiness and potential and to creating a road map for the campaign to come, they provide perceptions about how the constituency views the school—its strengths and weaknesses, its public image, its past successes, and special challenges to come.

Most often, fund-raising consultants conduct feasibility studies. Because they are outsiders, these consultants bring objectivity to the task and offer confidentiality to the interviewees. Because they are experienced, they bring special skills both to the interview and to an evaluation of the results.

The study begins with confidential interviews of 30 to 60 top potential donors and volunteers. Before being interviewed, participants receive a summary of the case for support. At the interview, the consultant asks for opinions and advice. Participants see a table of gifts needed to achieve the working goal and are asked to predict what their own level of commitment will be.

The consultant makes it clear that the interview is not a solicitation. However, it does serve as pre-campaign cultivation, as an introduction to the case for support, and as a personal preview of things to come.

When the interviews are finished, the consultant evaluates the findings and makes recommendations regarding all aspects of the upcoming campaign, including—most importantly—an appropriate gift table and goal.

Gift tables include a top gift that is at least 10 percent of the goal. In past decades, the tables have been based upon the rule of thirds. According to that, the top 10 donors contribute one-third of the goal, the next 100 donors account for the second third, and the balance comes from all other gifts. However, in more recent years, fewer donors have made larger gifts. At some institutions, for example, as few as 10 donors contribute 80 to 90 percent of the total raised. (See a sample gift table on page 81.)

Volunteers and staff can use gift tables during the actual solicitation. As Curtis F. Baggett wrote in *A Development Handbook: Promoting Philanthropy at Independent Schools* (CASE, 1992), "When a prospect wants to know how large a gift is expected, the solicitor can point to a line on the table and reply: 'I'm asking you to consider a gift in this range.' "

THE CAMPAIGN PLAN

The planning process is invaluable for building consensus for what will happen, when, and how.

The campaign plan provides a summary of what is to come for board review and approval and serves as a guide for staff and volunteers.

In the plan, which is informed by the feasibility study report, campaign decisions are documented and issues resolved. (See a sample plan's contents page on page 82.) The most important components relate to the people, the goal, the timetable, the cost, the policies, and the look.

The People

Two categories of people are essential to the success of a capital campaign: those who give and those who ask for gifts.

Those who give must be sufficiently numerous and must include some who are willing and able to make the top gifts. Capital campaigns, be they large or small, depend upon leadership gifts. Without those gifts, the entire effort has little chance for success. It is a well-established principle of capital fund raising that a school should be able to identify at least three viable prospects for every gift listed on the gift table.

The second key category of people is the fund-raising volunteers. During a capital campaign, schools assemble bigger and better cadres of volunteers who will improve the quality of the development program not only during the campaign but for many years to come.

Leading the volunteers is the campaign chair, an important participant who should be enlisted early in the campaign planning process. Through his or her words and deeds, the chair (or co-chairs) sets the tone for the entire campaign. Therefore, he or she should have:

- Stature and influence within the school community.
- Close ties to the school.
- A strong commitment to the cause.
- Leadership skills that will make it possible to enlist and motivate volunteers.
- Communication skills that will help to generate enthusiasm for the drive.
- Ample time to commit to the task.
- The ability and willingness to make a leadership gift and to seek leadership support from peers.

Both the chair and the committee members deserve written job descriptions that describe what they are expected to do and when. For example, at one school, the major gift committee members were told during the recruitment process that they would be expected to:

- Work as solicitors during the upcoming school year.
- Attend a pre-solicitation training session.
- Have strategy conversations with the director of development and a fellow solicitor prior to each solicitation.
- Attend four committee meetings.
- Solicit five to 10 top prospects in teams of two.
- Make an early individual or family pledge that reflects the philanthropic priority they attach to the campaign and that will serve as an example to other leadership donors.

At many schools, experienced development staff members also participate in gift solicitation, usually with a volunteer but occasionally alone. These staff members add to a meeting with a prospective donor a deep knowledge of the school and the campaign, as well as planned giving expertise.

The Goal

As Richard Page Allen wrote in *The Successful Capital Campaign: From Planning to Victory Celebration* (CASE, 1986), "An underlying rule of any fund-raising campaign is that it must be successful. People like winning teams. Failure to meet campaign goals will reduce enthusiasm for the institution."

Most well-planned campaigns achieve their goals. That's quite an amazing feat. One school sets a goal of $5 million and raises $5,100,000. Another school sets a goal of $50 million and raises $50,100,000. How do they do it? Setting achievable goals requires two steps.

1. The feasibility study report recommends a goal that is low enough to be realistic but high enough to inspire stretch gifts.
2. The school tests and confirms the feasibility study's recommended goal during a quiet advance-leadership-gifts phase. The purpose of the advance-leadership-gifts phase is to raise a nucleus fund consisting of 50 percent to 70 percent of the campaign goal. Only when this amount has been pledged is it time to publicly announce a campaign goal and timetable.

According to Henry D. Sharpe Jr. in *The Successful Capital Campaign (CASE, 1986)*, the final goal "is a moral statement. It is the embodiment of a reasoned and emotionally felt commitment by a caring leadership group to raise the sum they have carefully evaluated, understood, and now accepted."

Timetables

Capital campaigns have four phases:

1. *Getting ready:* Defining the institutional needs and developing the case.
2. *Getting set:* Conducting the feasibility study.

3. *Testing the waters:* Soliciting advance leadership gifts.
4. *Going public:* Announcing the goal and conducting the public campaign.

Typically, it takes one to two years to get ready and to get set, and one year to test the waters. The public phase that follows may span two years. However, within the independent school world, there are wide variations from those norms. Some schools do "quick and dirty" capital campaigns during which they raise large sums from relatively few donors and in a short time. Other schools require a decade from the definition of institutional needs to the announcement of fund-raising success.

According to educational campaign standards that CASE has adopted, the total period of campaign fund raising should not exceed seven years, including the advance gifts and the public phases but not the pre-campaign planning phase. That time period may work at a large college or university. However, at most independent schools, letting active solicitation of large groups go on for more than four years will drain momentum and eventually wear out both volunteers and staff.

Before a campaign begins, the staff should plot it on a calendar to indicate who will do what, when, where, and how. Campaign calendars give context and structure to the campaign. They assure the coordination of activities, meetings, deadlines, and events.

When schools seek capital funds for a new facility, one question always arises: "When should construction begin?" Starting early in the campaign may save costs. However, starting early is sure to discourage subsequent gifts. Those in charge of construction timetables should remember the words of Maurice G. Gurin in *Confessions of a Fund Raiser* (The Taft Group, 1985): "One doesn't have to be a professional fund raiser to know that it is very difficult to make the case for a need when it has practically been satisfied."

Campaign Costs

Independent school campaign costs average 5 to 10 percent of the total gifts received. However, the range is wide. Some campaigns cost as little as 3 percent; some cost as much as 20 percent.

This wide range is attributable to significant variations in (1) the size of the campaign goal, (2) the size and experience of the campaign staff, (3) the extent to which the school uses consultants, (4) the length of the campaign, and (5) the base of community support the school will seek. (Obviously, nationwide campaigns are more expensive than those that are locally based.)

Furthermore, because the school will encounter certain fixed costs irrespective of the goal, campaigns with smaller goals must budget costs as a higher percentage of the goal, while campaigns with larger goals can take advantage of economies of scale. (See a sample budget format on page 83.)

In the past, some independent schools with small development staffs have significantly increased the cost of their campaigns by employing two consultants. The first is a senior member of the consulting firm who conducts the feasibility study and provides on-site advice one or two days per month during the campaign. The second is a junior member of the firm who serves as resident consultant, managing the day-to-day work of the campaign in house.

However, as Charles P. Ries of The Oram Group noted in the May 1995 *Fund Raising Management* magazine, "Using consultants as temporary workers is, with a few exceptions, a poor investment.... The growing and maturing ranks of fund-raising professionals (is) making this practice obsolete." Today, most independent schools rely upon a senior consultant for guidance and manage the campaign with employees of their own.

In planning a campaign budget, it is wise to remember that today's donors are particularly responsive to cost-effective campaigns. These donors want their gifts used for construction rather than for parties and brochures. For that reason, all schools have become cost-conscious. Some seek one or more early gifts to cover fund-raising costs so that during subsequent solicitations they can say, "Every dollar you give will be used to support the goals of this campaign."

The Policies

"I'd like to name an endowment fund. How large must my gift be?"
"I'd like to contribute $100,000, but I'd have to pay it over seven years."

Many questions like these emerge during a capital campaign. Therefore, it's important to establish campaign policies that volunteer leaders and staff have carefully considered, the board has approved, and everyone soliciting gifts understands. The following is a sample of such policies from one school.

1. **The purpose of gifts.** Pledges or gifts will be credited to the campaign only if they are unrestricted or restricted to a campaign purpose. Pledges and gifts for other purposes are welcome and will be recognized but will not be credited to the campaign. (See a sample letter of intent on page 84.)

2. **The counting of deferred gifts.** Deferred gifts irrevocably pledged or transferred (i.e., the principal of a charitable remainder trust) during the campaign will be credited at their discounted present value, as computed under the applicable IRS actuarial table.

3. **The setting of a final goal.** A final goal and timetable will be set following the advance-leadership-gifts phase of the campaign and not until approximately two-thirds of the total has been pledged.

4. **The definition of a pledge period.** Pledges may be paid over three to five years. All pledges must be paid by a fixed future date.

5. **The treatment of annual gifts.** Annual giving will be maintained as a separate drive with a separate goal throughout the capital campaign.

When developing campaign policies, it is particularly important that staff and volunteer leaders establish guidelines regarding deferred gifts (Item 2 above) in advance of the campaign. The options are threefold: (a) credit the gift at the discounted present value as stated above, (b) credit the gift at its face amount (that is, without discount), or (c) credit only cash or other assets provided by a deferred gift, if and when they are received during the duration of the campaign.

Crediting a deferred gift, such as a charitable remainder trust funded with $200,000 at its face value ($200,000), may appear to be a donor-friendly policy. However, doing so also provides an inflated and unrealistic impression of the value of the gift because it assumes that the school has the funds right away, even though that is not the case. On the other hand, crediting the gift at its present value reflects the value to the school today of what the funds will be worth when they are received at a future date. To calculate a present value, the trust principal must be reduced by the value of income the school would have received had it had the trust principal to invest during the years between the date of the funding of the trust and the date on which the principal is received.

In addition to policies regarding gifts, campaign leaders should establish and the board should approve policies for solicitors and donors. For example:

- Each trustee will make his or her pledge during the first few months of the campaign.
- No solicitor will seek a gift until he or she has made a pledge.
- All solicitations for gifts over $10,000 will be made in person and by two solicitors who have met with an appropriate staff member in advance to rehearse the conversation they will have.

The Look

Campaign publicity gives wide visibility to the capital needs of a school and enhances the climate for giving constituency-wide. Press releases, publications, videos, and special events offer important opportunities to increase community awareness of the institutional mission, to explain the current need, to establish donor confidence in the campaign's success, to keep solicitors on task, and to recognize important gifts.

Campaign publicity should begin with good in-house communication. Faculty, staff, and students should be informed about a capital campaign before it begins and should receive regular updates while it lasts.

Furthermore, even though campaign publicity is community-wide, everyone should remember that top prospects are key. The school should send its newsletters, letters, and invitations to them first, accompanied by a personal note. At every step of the way, top prospects should be informed as insiders and treated as valued friends.

WHAT HAPPENS TO ANNUAL GIVING DURING A CAPITAL CAMPAIGN?

The good news: Annual gifts almost always increase during a capital campaign.

Many schools keep annual and capital giving separate and distinct during a capital campaign.

However, during the 1990s, more independent schools have followed the lead of colleges and universities and characterized their capital campaigns as "total voluntary support," counting both annual and capital gifts made during the period of the campaign. By including annual gifts, these schools are able to offer all donors, large and small, the opportunity to participate in the capital campaign. And, of course, the schools are also able to set a higher goal.

Whether or not they count annual giving in the capital campaign goal, all schools should emphasize the key differences between the two appeals. "We depend," they should explain, "upon annual giving for operating revenue. And if annual giving is to grow, we must have widespread support by habitual donors educated to increase the size of their gifts each year.

"On the other hand, capital campaigns to meet special capital purposes and endowment needs occur perhaps once every eight to 10 years. During these campaigns, our most capable potential donors are asked to make significant gifts in addition to their annual support."

Regardless of whether annual giving remains separate or is bundled into a capital campaign goal, it is likely to increase during the campaign years. This is due to the fact that:

- During a campaign, the school's needs for voluntary support have greater visibility and broader appeal. There is widespread publicity about and more enthusiasm for the process of seeking and making gifts. More previous non-donors make first annual gifts. Lapsed donors may give again.
- During a campaign, more gifts are sought in person, often in the form of a joint annual and capital appeal. Personal solicitation always fosters increased levels of support.

Tax-Exempt Bonds and Fund Raising

Since the 1990s, tax-exempt bonds have become the debt vehicle of choice for independent schools. Tax-exempt bonds are widely advertised as the lowest-cost financing available.

Many boards of trustees, even the traditionally debt-averse, have determined that their schools will be financially stronger in the years to come if they borrow on a tax-exempt basis for capital projects.

In general, tax-exempt bonds are issued for facilities projects only, and very often they come with significant restrictions on fund raising. Therefore, it is wise for a school to make the decision to acquire a tax-exempt bond *before* planning capital fund raising so that the leadership can take such restrictions into account.

For example, bonding agencies often insist that a school cannot raise money for the same project for which it is floating a bond. Therefore, the school must seek campaign pledges and gifts in the form of unrestricted contributions to a development fund even though, in spirit, the gifts are in support of the specific new facilities. In other words, funds to construct a new gym must be sought and contributed as "unrestricted" gifts even though the school may offer donors naming opportunities within the new gym in recognition of their general support.

In recent years, some schools have regarded tax-exempt bonds as a bonanza. After all, with a bond, a school can borrow at a tax-exempt interest rate and keep its unrestricted campaign proceeds and endowment invested at taxable rates. It can build badly needed facilities at once, possibly increasing the likelihood of generous gifts from current parents and surely spreading the cost among future generations of parents. At the same time, the school can focus more on endowment fund raising.

However, debt is debt, no matter how it is costumed. Individual boards must consider their schools' capacity for and comfort with debt, particularly in light of the long-term tradeoffs that arise when the operating budget has a substantial debt-service line item for decades to come.

Furthermore, bonds are complicated and expensive to arrange. Costs can run from $100,000 to $200,000 and are unrelated to the amount being bonded. One of a bond's hidden costs is that someone at the school must fill out a mountain of forms and create many new documents. The process is quite slow, requiring visits from and to banks and lawyers. The school must do a great deal of new financial analysis and employ an expert bond attorney.

Therefore, the board of trustees should weigh the pros and cons of tax-exempt bonds and make a decision before designing a capital campaign. Too many schools have had to discard expensive campaign materials because the bonding agency deemed the fund-raising literature inappropriate! Others should learn from these unfortunate experiences.

THE ONGOING VS. THE TRADITIONAL CAMPAIGN

Some schools have abandoned the traditional capital campaign in favor of a capital gifts program that is ongoing and low-key. Proponents of this approach argue that:

- An ongoing campaign is donor-focused. It permits the solicitation of gifts when the time is right for the donor rather than the school.
- An ongoing campaign is less pressured. There is no need to complete solicitations by a certain date, so there is more time to contemplate planned gifts.
- An ongoing campaign has no public goals or timetables, so there is no risk of failure.
- An ongoing campaign is less exhausting for the school head and permits the staff and volunteers to pace themselves from year to year.

On the other hand, the traditional campaign has clear advantages as well.

- It provides an occasion, a moment in time, around which the board, administration, staff, and volunteers can rally and to which donors can respond.
- It is almost always preceded by improved donor research, accelerated donor cultivation, and an increase in professionalism on the part of the development staff.
- Its visible timetable and goals create a sense of urgency and momentum and foster more widespread support and more generous gifts.

Whichever approach schools choose, one thing is clear. In the decades to come, all schools that wish to make the most of their voluntary support will solicit major gifts every year irrespective of whether they do so in lieu of or between campaigns.

All schools with sophisticated development programs will focus more time on the major donor—on his or her timetable and fiscal needs and on his or her philanthropic interests and intent. Only in this way will schools be able to meet their increased needs for voluntary support.

MEASURING SUCCESS

The campaign has ended; the goal has been reached. However, that's not the only measure of campaign success. A successful campaign should achieve these ancillary goals as well:

- It should upgrade donors and enlarge the major donor base.
- It should give the entire development program a major gifts focus.
- It should broaden and strengthen the volunteer corps and improve the school head's fund-raising skills.

- It should lead to the establishment of better development systems and methods and a more professional development staff.

As the celebration proceeds, those responsible for campaign success should understand that they have achieved much more than a fiscal goal, and far more than an increased endowment and new gym. In a very real sense, they have laid the groundwork for major gift fund-raising success for many decades to come.

What a Feasibility Study Provides

Findings: Opinions, Perceptions, and Intentions

About the School
- Present image
- Strengths
- Weaknesses
- Future prospects

About the Case for Support
- Priority capital needs
- Identified capital projects
- Architectural plans
- Role of endowment

About Individual Donors
- Place of school among philanthropic priorities
- Present capital campaign gift intentions
- Future gift intentions
- Identification of other prospects
- Evaluation of other prospects

About the Campaign
- Achievability of goal
- Timeliness
- Duration
- Potential leadership
- Potential solicitors

About the Wider Community
- Economic conditions
- Competitive fund raising by other organizations
- Sources of foundation and corporation support

Recommendations

About the Campaign Goal
- Dollar amount
- Number, range, and size of gifts

About the Case for Support
- Components
- Emphasis
- Presentation

About the Campaign Timetable
- Planning and preparation schedule
- Public relations schedule
- Leadership gifts schedule
- General solicitation schedule

About Pre-campaign Activities
- Prospect research
- Donor identification
- Donor cultivation
- Campaign plan
- Statement of case

About the Campaign Organization
- Overall structure
- Individual committees
- Leadership roles
- Number and categories of volunteers
- Role of the board of trustees
- Campaign publications and events

About Campaign Strategies
- Recruitment of volunteers
- Training of volunteers
- Solicitation of prospects
- Commemorative gift opportunities
- Recognition of donors
- Stewardship of donors

About the Overall Institutional Image
- Present opportunities
- Long-range ramifications

THE REYNOLDS SCHOOL
$10,000,000 Capital Campaign

Working Table of Gifts Used During Feasibility Study

# of Prospects	# Gifts	Gift Range	Total	Running Total
3	1	$1,000,000	$1,000,000	$ 1,000,000
3	1	$750,000	$ 750,000	$ 1,750,000
6	2	$500,000	$1,000,000	$ 2,750,000
12	4	$250,000	$1,000,000	$ 3,750,000
36	12	$100,000	$1,200,000	$ 4,950,000
60	20	$75,000	$1,500,000	$ 6,450,000
90	30	$50,000	$1,500,000	$ 7,950,000
120	40	$25,000	$1,000,000	$ 8,950,000
225	75	$10,000	$750,000	$ 9,700,000
Many		Under $10,000	$300,000	$10,000,000

THE REYNOLDS SCHOOL

Capital Campaign Plan
Table of Contents

Premises and Purposes

Timetable

Goal Setting and Sharing

Campaign Organization

Campaign Leadership and Job Descriptions

Table of Gifts Needed

Named Gift Opportunities

Gift Acceptance and Crediting Policies

Solicitation Guidelines

Campaign Communications and Events

Case Statement

Solicitation Stages and Phases

The Role of Annual Giving

The Role of Planned Giving

The Role of the Board of Trustees

Campaign Budget

THE REYNOLDS SCHOOL
Three-Year Capital Campaign Budget Format

Campaign Director — $_____

Printing
Case statement, supporting brochures,
training materials, stationery, pledge cards,
invitations, forms, etc. — $_____

Postage
For all purposes — $_____

Design Services
Publication design, photography — $_____

Consulting Services — $_____

Feasibility Study — $_____

Cultivation and Stewardship
Major donor individual and group entertaining — $_____

Travel
Cultivation and solicitation visits to
major prospects and for group meetings
of the school head and volunteers — $_____

Office Supplies and Equipment — $_____

Publicity
Campaign newsletters, press relations — $_____

Special Events
Kickoff ceremony, catering services — $_____

Plaques, Mementos — $_____

Major Donor Research Services — $_____

Contingency — $_____

TOTAL — $_____

THE REYNOLDS SCHOOL
Capital Campaign Letter of Intent*

In consideration of the gifts of others and to assist in meeting the needs of The Reynolds School, I/we hereby pledge $_____ to the school's capital campaign.

I/we have enclosed $ _____. Subsequent pledge payments will be made ____annually _____semi-annually _____quarterly _____monthly

This pledge will be fully paid by this date:_____

My/our gift is ☐ Unrestricted
☐ Designated for capital improvements
☐ Designated for endowment
☐ In honor of or in memory of:

_____

This pledge is binding upon my estate.

Name_____

(please print)

_____

Signature_____

Date_____

Name_____

(please print)

_____

Signature_____

Date_____

Address_____

_____

City_____ State_____ ZIP_____

Reminders will be generated in accordance with the schedule you have provided.
* The language in this letter of intent must be altered if the school is using tax-exempt bond financing.

CHAPTER EIGHT

PLANNED GIVING

FRED FISKE AND THE NEWEST
FUND-RAISING FRONTIER

"I can't tell you how grateful I am to your school. The education is so active, so energizing, so different from mine many years ago. My grandchildren have blossomed and flourished and thrived. But it's those grandchildren I care about now. I wish I could give you a major gift, but I want my life savings to go to them."

Robert and Roberta Jones, ages 74 and 70, are the grandparents of three students at an independent school. Mr. Jones spoke those kind words during a solicitation for a capital campaign leadership gift.

The solicitor reported to the school's director of development, Fred Fiske, "Mr. Jones said he couldn't make a gift, but he and his wife love the school. I think we might work out something just for them."

Something just for them. That's what planned giving is all about.

Planned giving is a market-oriented approach to fund raising. A planned gift helps the donor as well as the school. The donor reduces taxes, increases income, or satisfies another personal financial need. The school receives a significant gift, often a gift of property such as stock, real estate, or a residence.

Planned gifts are made when the donor is ready, when the time and gift vehicle fit an individual donor's circumstances and needs. For example, he or she may decide to make such a gift while reviewing an estate plan or when anticipating retirement.

Planned gifts are made to schools that market planned giving options—schools that educate their constituents about planned gift opportunities and build close relationships with those in their community to whom those gifts are most likely to appeal.

Many planned gifts are deferred. They provide a financial benefit to the school only when a trust terminates or a donor dies. However, planned gifts also can provide current income to the school. They can help the school today.

For these reasons, increasing numbers of independent schools have added planned giving as a complement to their annual and capital fund drives.

To attract significant voluntary support, schools must offer their potential donors:

- the opportunity to serve personal financial needs,
- the opportunity to combine current and deferred support, and
- the same array of appealing gift opportunities offered by other nonprofit institutions that those same donors support.

WHY PLANNED GIFTS ARE RIGHT FOR SCHOOLS

In her book, *Targeted Fund Raising* (Precept Press, 1994), Judith E. Nichols identifies characteristics of institutions that can successfully seek planned gifts. These institutions have:

- a large number of older donors,
- a large number of consistent annual donors, and
- a perception among potential donors that the organization has made a meaningful difference in their lives.

Independent schools have older donors, particularly among their alumni, parents of alumni, and grandparents; they know who those older donors are and that some are affluent. Independent schools have annual giving programs that have attracted loyal supporters, and they know who those supporters are. Furthermore, independent schools make a significant difference in the lives of those they serve. Therefore, the case for a planned giving program is often strong and clear.

Even so, many schools, including some with sophisticated development programs, have held back from this fund-raising frontier. Why do they resist? Three reasons stand out.

1. *The financial benefits of a planned gift are often delayed.* Some planned gifts provide immediate income, but many, such as bequests, life insurance, and charitable remainder trusts, do not. The school must allocate staff time today even though it may not receive any benefit for years. Some boards feel

that their development staffs should focus on fund raising that produces immediate cash.

2. *The solicitation of a planned gift often takes a long time.* An annual gift may require one letter and one call. A capital gift may take one to three visits to close. However, it may take more than a year to complete a planned gift. Typically, the donor's attorney or financial adviser becomes involved. Over time, the large potential of planned giving is clear, but it may not be cost-effective at the start.

3. *Planned giving intimidates the development staff.* Usually, the director of development must assume responsibility for a planned giving program until the value of adding a planned giving officer becomes clear. Most directors of development understand the importance of planned gifts, but many fear that planned giving is too complex to learn or too technical to understand.

HOW CAN I MARKET PLANNED GIFTS?

At Fred Fiske's school, the pressure for a planned giving program came from the board. At first Fred was not enthusiastic about the idea.

"I don't know anything about gift taxes and remainder trusts," he said. "How can I market planned gifts?"

During the next few years, Fred learned that planned giving need not be complex. Quite simply, it offers the prospective donor five principal options in addition to a gift of cash or marketable securities. A donor who wishes to make a $100,000 gift can:

- Give $100,000 to the school now and retain investment income from that gift during his or her life, or during the life of a spouse, or during both lives. Thereafter, the principal passes to the school.
- "Lend" $100,000 to the school for a specified period. The school receives the annual income, after which the principal typically passes to a child or grand-child.
- Give the school assets it can sell for $100,000. Many schools have received gifts of silver, stamp collections, land, houses, and even horses with a value of $100,000 or much more.
- Leave the school $100,000 by will.
- Make the school the owner and beneficiary of a $100,000 life insurance policy.

Fred became skilled at identifying prospective donors who might be interested in a planned gift. He and his volunteer solicitors learned that most often the best prospect for a planned gift wants to support the school and also has one or more of these specific desires:

- To reduce or avoid taxes (signaled by a statement such as, "I wish I could sell my farm, but I'd have to pay such a large capital gains tax").
- To increase income at retirement. ("Yes, I do have all that stock, but the dividends are so small.")
- To pass assets on to children or grandchildren. ("Unfortunately, my own children can't afford to send their children to college; it's going to be up to me.")
- To turn non-liquid assets into cash. ("All my money is in my business. I'd rather have some of it in my bank.")

That's all the solicitor has to know to identify planned gift prospects and to refer them to the development staff. For those who want more specific details, Fred prepared the planned giving primers that appear at the end of this chapter. (See pages 94–97.)

In discussing planned gifts with his volunteers, Fred focused on the importance of seeking the outright gift first whenever possible. As William F. Dailey wrote in *The Successful Capital Campaign* (CASE, 1986), "I have seen a lot of potential gift money 'left on the table' because a staff person opted for a deferred gift approach with a prospect who was perfectly capable of making a comparable outright gift."

THE FIRST STEP
To get off to a good start, development officers need to lay the groundwork with the right training, technical advice, and tools.

To launch a planned giving program, what Fred Fiske needed first was time—time he previously spent doing something else. His school head understood; she knew that without a significant time commitment, Fred could achieve little. Therefore, she added a part-time staff member and asked Fred to devote 20 percent of his time to planned giving.

Second, Fred needed to educate himself.

Through the National Committee on Planned Giving and CASE, he located seminars for beginners. He read clear, simple books. He joined a planned giving study group in his community. He purchased user-friendly computer software that helped him understand and design planned gifts. He contacted planned giving consultants who offer brochures and educational newsletters that he could adapt and personalize for his school.

During the planned giving program's initial year, with the help of his school head and the development committee of his board, Fred formed a six-member planned giving committee. Its members—all volunteers—were attorneys, bank officers, and financial planners who agreed to provide their services without cost. They met with Fred to discuss gift vehicles and to critique proposed gifts. When appropriate, they met with potential donors. (However, they always advised potential donors to consult their own attorneys and financial advisors as well.) And, as a first step, each member of the committee made his or her own planned gift.

Third, Fred's school launched The 1920 Society to honor all individuals who included the school in their estate plans.

The society was so named because 1920 was the year of the school's founding. To join, prospective members had to notify Fred that they had included the school in their estate plan. An acceptable bequest had to be of a specified amount or a specified percentage of the estate. Life insurance and other benefits at death were also acceptable.

Bequests, Fred soon learned, would be both the easiest component of the program to market and the most likely to have widespread appeal. And over time in the aggregate, they would provide an important return. Even colleges and universities with decades-old planned giving programs find that 80 percent of the endowment principal comes from bequests.

Some schools ask bequest society members to provide evidence of their charitable intent by photocopying or repeating in a letter the exact language from a will, trust, or life insurance policy. Fred's planned giving committee recommended that the school seek that evidence or proof at a later date, when the time appeared right. At the outset, the committee wanted to build the society's membership, something donors were more likely to do if it were relatively simple to join.

The school announced the founding of The 1920 Society at a dinner to which the oldest alumni were invited and at which the school head reported that every trustee had already included the school in his or her estate plan.

Thereafter, Fred publicized The 1920 Society whenever and wherever he could: in the school's quarterly magazine, in the annual fund brochure, in the school's year-end giving reminder, and in simple brochures he sent out to selected prospects every few months. Members of The 1920 Society received a handsome certificate. They were promised invitations to special planned giving seminars and acknowledgment in perpetuity in the school's annual report.

By the end of its second year, The 1920 Society at Fred's school had 75 members. Two had died, and the school was due to receive almost $100,000 from their estates. Among those 75 members were several who had not previously expressed an interest in the school.

NEVER UNDERESTIMATE A BEQUEST

An experienced planned giving officer told Fred never to underestimate the importance of a bequest because:

- *Bequests can provide large gifts to small or young schools.* Many schools receive the largest gift in their history in the form of a bequest.

- *Bequests can be upgraded to lifetime gifts.* Every donor who commits to a bequest is indicating that he or she cares deeply about a school's mission and goals. Therefore, all promised bequests should be welcomed, even those from alumni who are very young. When properly cultivated over time, these prospects, who are signaling their strong interest in the school, may upgrade their commitments to a lifetime gift.

- *For the donor, a bequest is a gift today.* Even though a school may not receive the financial benefit for a very long time, from the donor's point of view, a bequest is a meaningful commitment from the moment he or she notifies the school about it. Therefore, it's important to treat a bequest notification as a gift deserving of immediate gratitude, recognition, and praise.

THE NEXT STEPS

Too often, planned giving efforts fail because the development staff doesn't have time to respond to expressions of interest.

Once launched, the school's planned giving initiative also included several short, simple brochures. Each described in non-technical terms a different planned gift that could benefit a donor and the school. Each contained a confidential reply card for those seeking more information or a personal meeting to discuss a gift.

The brochures were targeted at groups to whom the gifts described were likely to have the most appeal. For example, one brochure educated younger alumni about the low annual cost of buying insurance and naming the school as beneficiary and owner of the policy. Another informed older, more affluent alumni about the benefits of a charitable remainder trust.

The school mailed brochures to only 25 to 50 carefully selected prospects at a time so that Fred would be able to follow up promptly as he received replies. Too often, planned giving initiatives fail because the development director receives an expression of interest but is unable to respond. Planned giving, like all major gift fund raising, is about building personal relationships. Anyone who returns a confidential reply card is inviting a relationship; he or she must hear from the development office at once!

Selected planned gift prospects were invited to attend an evening seminar at the school. At these seminars, experts (including planned giving officers from higher education) discussed the advantages of a variety of planned gift vehicles from the donor's point of view. One seminar was for grandparents alone. Another one that assumed a rudimentary knowledge of planned gifts was for attorneys, accountants, stockbrokers, trust officers, and fiscal planners in the school's community.

WHAT THE 2001 TAX ACT MAY MEAN

Many prospects may wonder about the Economic Growth and Tax Relief Reconciliation Act of 2001, which has been widely characterized as bad news for charities. In particular, the phasing-down of the estate tax between 2002 and 2009 and its full repeal as of 2010 have been highlighted by lobbyists who opposed the act prior to its enactment and by numerous reports in the press thereafter.

Schools would be wise to focus on the following important facts about the new law:

- The advantages of lifetime charitable giving continue. Furthermore, the decrease in the tax incentive for charitable bequests may increase the motivation for lifetime giving.
- There will be a continuing income tax advantage to designating a school as the post-mortem beneficiary of an IRA, 401(k), or other qualified plan benefit.
- At least until 2010, a substantial estate tax will be in effect and therefore charitable bequests at death will continue to generate an estate tax savings.
- The very absence of an estate tax at a future date may encourage some donors to make more rather than less generous charitable gifts. In 2010 and thereafter, should there be no estate tax, wealthy donors will be able to leave almost twice as much to their family as they can do today. This may motivate them to share a part of that increase with the charitable causes they support.
- Finally, all of the observations above assume that the new Act will not be repealed or amended. That assumption is far from a certainty.

OTHER WAYS TO GIVE

Fred learned that some donors, rather than making gifts directly, prefer to give through other charitable organizations. In particular, he became familiar with:

1. The Private Foundation

A private foundation is a charitable organization typically funded and controlled by an individual and his or her family, or by a corporation. Funds held in a private foundation have already been irrevocably committed to charity with attendant tax benefits. However, the foundation's officers and directors are able to decide, on an annual basis, which charities (including independent schools) they wish to support. By law, private foundation grants are a matter of public record.

2. The Donor-Advised Fund

A donor-advised fund, unlike a private foundation, is a charitable organization that receives widespread public support. However, it segregates for accounting purposes the contributions of each donor and permits each one to specify which charitable organizations (including independent schools) should receive his or her contributions, how much to give, and when to give it. Gifts made through donor-advised funds are not a matter of public record.

3. The Supporting Foundation

A supporting foundation is a private foundation that is closely aligned with and financially aids a specific charity, such as an independent school. The benefited school or other organization usually has a majority voice on the supporting foundation's board. The donor who establishes a supporting foundation typically is a member of the foundation board because he or she wishes to play an ongoing role in the management of the foundation and the awarding of grants.

MR. AND MRS. JONES MAKE A PLANNED GIFT

A well-designed planned gift can help a school, a donor, and the donors' heirs.

Within a year, more than 100 carefully targeted prospects at Fred Fiske's school had received a brochure and/or an invitation to a school-sponsored seminar. Eleven prospects had sent in confidential reply cards. Fred visited with each of these 11 prospects even though once or twice he had to travel out of town.

Mr. and Mrs. Jones were among the first to receive a brochure, and Mr. Jones was the very first to reply. He and Mrs. Jones made a significant planned gift that helped the school at once.

Included in their investment portfolio were $2 million in long-term government bonds purchased several years ago. These bonds generated annual interest of 7 percent, or $110,000 per year. Mr and Mrs. Jones put the $2 million in bonds in a trust and named their bank as trustee. The trust instrument directed the trustee to pay the school an annuity of $140,000 per year for each of the next 10 years. At the end of 10 years, the trust was to terminate. The principal would then be available for the grandchildren to pay college tuition, to begin a new career, to buy a first house, or to save and invest.

As a result:

- The school would receive $140,000 a year for 10 consecutive years, for a total of $1,400,000.
- Ten years hence, the Jones grandchildren would receive the $2 million in bonds (in trust for those who were still too young to receive the assets outright).
- Mr. and Mrs. Jones would avoid a gift tax or estate tax of approximately $300,000, the amount they would have been required to pay had they given the bonds to their grandchildren (or their grandchildren's trust) directly in their lifetime or by will.

Several months later, a feature article about Mr. and Mrs. Jones and their decision to make a significant planned gift appeared in the school's quarterly magazine. Fred sent an advance copy to the Joneses with this note:

"Not only have you made a generous gift to your grandchildren's school, but you have also set a wonderful example that many others will follow in future years. We will always think of you with gratitude as our school's planned giving pioneers!"

A Planned Giving Primer for Solicitors

How Mr. Generous Can Make a Gift:
Options and Examples

LIFETIME GIFTS

1. **Cash:** Mr. Generous sends a $5,000 check to the school.

2. **Appreciated securities:** Mr. Generous transfers to the school stock valued at $100,000 that he purchased for $25,000 more than one year ago.

3. **Tangible personal property:** Mr. Generous delivers a valuable painting to the school for display in the arts center or for the school to sell.

4. **Real estate:** Mr. Generous transfers a readily salable vacation home (acquired more than one year ago and with no mortgage or environmental hazards) to the school, or he transfers the home to the school but retains the right to occupy it for life.

5. **Life insurance policy:** Mr. Generous irrevocably assigns a life insurance policy to the school and each year contributes to the school an amount equal to the annual premium.

6. **Charitable lead trust:** Mr. Generous establishes a trust, transfers stock worth $2 million to the trust, and directs that the trust pay the school $140,000 each year for 15 years. After 15 years, the trust terminates and the remaining principal is distributed to his grandchildren.

7. **Charitable remainder trust:** Mr. Generous establishes a trust, transfers stock worth $2 million to the trust, and directs that the trust pay him or another designated beneficiary an annual payment of 7 percent of the principal, revalued each year, for life. Upon the beneficiary's death, the trust terminates and the principal is distributed to the school.

8. **Charitable gift annuity:** Mr. Generous transfers appreciated stock to the school in exchange for the school's agreement to pay a specified annuity to him, or another designated beneficiary, for life.

9. **Pooled income fund:** Mr. Generous transfers cash or securities to a trust fund, called a pooled income fund, that the school maintains for multiple donors. He reserves a pro rata share of the income from the trust fund for himself, or for another designated beneficiary, for life. Upon the beneficiary's death, a pro rata portion of the trust fund is distributed to the school.

A Planned Giving Primer for Solicitors

How Mr. Generous Can Make a Gift:
Options and Examples

ESTATE GIFTS

1. **Bequest:** Mr. Generous includes an outright bequest of $250,000 to the school in his will, or he leaves to the school by will a specified percentage of his estate.

2. **Life insurance proceeds:** Mr. Generous designates the school as the beneficiary of a life insurance policy that he owns on his own life.

3. **Charitable lead trust created by will:** Mr. Generous includes a provision in his will directing the transfer of $2 million in trust and providing an annual payment of $140,000 to the school for 15 years. At the end of the trust term, the principal is distributed to the donor's grandchildren.

4. **Charitable remainder trust created by will:** Mr. Generous includes a provision in his will directing the transfer of $2 million in trust and providing an annual payment of 7 percent of the principal, revalued annually, to his sibling or to another designated beneficiary. Upon the income beneficiary's death, the principal is distributed to the school.

5. **Charitable gift annuity acquired under direction by will:** Mr. Generous directs the executor of his will to transfer appreciated securities to the school in exchange for the school's agreement to pay a specified annuity for life to a beneficiary he designates.

6. **Qualified plan benefits:** Mr. Generous designates the school as the post-mortem lump sum beneficiary of any balance remaining in his qualified plan (IRA, 401(k) plan, pension, or profit-sharing plan) on his death or, alternatively, on the death of his wife if she survives him.

NOTE: Under the Tax Act of 2001, the estate tax will be gradually reduced until 2009 and eliminated as of 2010. The Act provides for the reinstatement of the estate tax in 2011. It is likely that the elimination, reinstatement, or both will be modified by future legislation, although the nature of such modifications cannot be predicted now.

A Planned Giving Primer for Solicitors

When Mr. Generous Makes a Gift:
Options and Donor Benefits

LIFETIME GIFTS

1. **Cash:** Mr. Generous receives an income-tax deduction and achieves estate-tax savings.

2. **Appreciated securities (held for more than one year):** Mr. Generous receives an income-tax deduction and achieves estate-tax savings. He also avoids a capital-gains tax on the appreciation.

3. **Tangible personal property:** Mr. Generous receives an income-tax deduction and achieves estate-tax savings.

4. **Real estate (held for more than one year):** Mr. Generous receives an income-tax deduction and achieves estate-tax savings. He also avoids a capital-gains tax on any appreciation.

5. *Life insurance policy:* Mr. Generous receives an income-tax deduction and achieves estate-tax savings.

6. **Charitable lead trust:** Mr. Generous provides the school with income during the term of the trust. This income is not subject to income tax. He also reduces the gift tax on an intra-family gift of assets that return to the family after the trust terminates. In addition, Mr. Generous achieves estate-tax savings.

7. **Charitable remainder trust:** Mr. Generous receives an income-tax deduction and achieves estate-tax savings. He avoids, or in some cases defers, a capital-gains tax on any sale by the trust of appreciated trust assets, and he provides himself, or another designated beneficiary, with income during the term of the trust.

8. **Charitable gift annuity:** Mr. Generous receives an income-tax deduction and achieves estate-tax savings. If the annuity is purchased with appreciated securities, he defers a capital-gains tax on the appreciation. In addition, he provides himself with income for life.

9. **Pooled income fund:** Mr. Generous receives an income-tax deduction and achieves estate-tax savings. If Mr. Generous transferred appreciated stock (as distinguished from cash) to the pooled income fund, he achieves investment diversification without incurring a capital-gains tax. Finally, Mr. Generous provides income for life for himself or another designated beneficiary.

A Planned Giving Primer for Solicitors

When Mr. Generous Makes a Gift:
Options and Donor Benefits

ESTATE GIFTS

1. **Bequest:** Mr. Generous achieves estate-tax savings.

2. **Life insurance proceeds:** Mr. Generous achieves estate-tax savings.

3. **Charitable lead trust created by will:** Mr. Generous achieves estate-tax savings and the assets are returned to his family when the trust terminates.

4. **Charitable remainder trust created by will:** Mr. Generous achieves estate-tax savings and provides a designated beneficiary with income for life.

5. **Charitable gift annuity acquired under direction by will:** Mr. Generous achieves estate-tax savings and provides a designated beneficiary with income for life.

6. **Qualified plan benefits:** Mr. Generous achieves estate-tax savings. Furthermore, had he designated a family member as the post-mortem lump-sum beneficiary, the family member would have had to pay an income tax on the benefit. The school pays no tax.

NOTE: Under the Tax Act of 2001, the estate tax will be gradually reduced until 2009 and eliminated as of 2010. The Act provides for the reinstatement of the estate tax in 2011. It is likely that the elimination, reinstatement, or both will be modified by future legislation, although the nature of such modifications cannot be predicted now.

CHAPTER NINE

THE RIGHT DEVELOPMENT DIRECTOR
Passion, Professionalism, and Pride

A planning system, no matter how good, does not guarantee success in fund raising. The system must be implemented by someone with a particular set of skills—the skills of a fund-raising professional.

—The Guaranteed Fund-Raising System
Dennis J. Murray (American Institute of Management, 1994)

A development director is an advocate, and the most effective advocates are passionate about their cause. A development director is a professional, and the best professionals have high standards, extensive knowledge, and a desire to learn even more. A development director is a leader and a follower, a teacher and a student.

Worthwhile though the challenge may be, it's not an easy job.

Some development directors remain at one school for 10 to 30 years. They're most likely to stay when they and their school heads share common values, similar ideals, and a commitment to fund-raising success. It also helps immensely when the school's trustees treat the development director with trust and respect.

However, throughout the nonprofit world, long tenure among chief advancement officers is increasingly rare. During the past few decades, independent school heads have searched for new development directors every two to four years on average. Why don't they stay longer? Several reasons stand out:

- **A poor fit.** Just as the right chemistry between the school head and development director makes fund-raising success possible, the wrong chemistry undermines effectiveness and makes the fund raiser dissatisfied with the job.
- **A wide choice.** More nonprofit organizations are hiring development officers every year. Opportunities for skilled, experienced professionals abound.
- **Higher salary.** Development directors' salaries have increased more slowly at independent schools than elsewhere in the nonprofit world. According to NAIS, in 2001-2002 the median salary for development directors was $68,256. Often skilled development professionals can earn more at another job.
- **Burnout.** Even the best development directors cannot meet every institutional need; schools must set priorities. But some heads, trustees, and fund-raising volunteers have unrealistic expectations about what a fund raiser can accomplish in a single school year. Their development directors try to please but, after a few years, feel used up.

As a result of these factors, each year there are many school heads in the market for a top-notch development professional. Occasionally they engage consulting firms to conduct the search. More commonly, they conduct the development search in house.

A search is especially inconvenient when a capital campaign is looming. But no matter what's happening in the life of the school, conducting a search is always a challenge. Even when applicants abound, qualified candidates are not easy to find.

THE IDEAL CANDIDATE
The best development directors have a broad mix of skills and nine important characteristics.

There is no one profile for the ideal candidate. To the contrary, top-notch independent school development directors have dissimilar resumes. Their educations are diverse; few took fund-raising courses when they were in college. Their work experiences are varied; few focused on development from the start of their careers.

Some come on board with in-depth knowledge of their schools, perhaps because they are alumni, parents, or current employees. Others have development expertise but must learn about the institutions they serve.

As in all jobs, relevant experience counts. A candidate who has managed annual and capital drives at a school has particular appeal. However, equally important are several characteristics that the best development officers share. These characteristics are:

1. *Creativity.* Talented development directors have initiative and a zest for new ideas. They focus first on fund-raising concepts (what are we trying to accomplish and why?) and only thereafter on fund-raising techniques (how are we going to do it and when?).

2. *Flexibility.* All directors of development have a multi-faceted job that requires working with a variety of people. That means they must fit themselves into the school environment and interact successfully with colleagues, trustees, and volunteer leaders. They must adapt and problem-solve every day.

3. *Communication skills.* Successful development directors communicate confidently and well. They speak effectively and persuasively. They write quickly and with ease.

4. *Eagerness to learn.* There are few college degrees in development, but there are many opportunities to learn. The best development directors continue to learn throughout their careers. They seek opportunities and set aside time for professional growth.

5. *The ability to lead.* Good development directors enjoy a leadership role and know how to build consensus. Staff members are happy to be on their team.

6. *Deep feelings for the school.* An appropriate development director believes deeply in the school's mission and is eager to further its goals.

7. *A passion for detail.* In development, success or failure is often in the details. Records must be accurate; names must be correct; gift acknowledgments must be prompt. The best development directors are computer-literate, careful, and consistent.

The Well-Crafted Job Description

The first step: writing a job description to summarize in ads and share with candidates. The description should include the following:

- School history, mission, and future plans.
- School development program—its scope, its past record, and its present goals.
- Development office budget and staff.

- Experience and skills that are prerequisites for the job.
- Compensation package—the salary range and the benefits package.
- Procedure for applicants and the date on which he or she should begin.

8. *Comfort behind the scenes.* Effective development directors are happy to let others take credit for fund-raising success. They are content to remain in the background and to lead the applause.

9. *Commitment to the job.* Development directors work hard. They are dedicated to their jobs, their programs, their staffs, and their volunteers. When necessary, they come in early and stay late.

CONDUCTING THE SEARCH

Time-consuming as it is, the search process is too important to allow for short cuts.

Because networking is often the easiest way to find appropriate and experienced candidates, most school heads begin a search by consulting their peers. A letter to fellow school heads and to development directors at nearby educational institutions (including colleges and universities) might conclude: "If you know anyone who meets our qualifications and who may be interested in a challenging career at our school, please ask him or her to contact me directly." (See a sample letter on page 106.)

It is also worthwhile to place advertisements in local fund-raising and planned giving newsletters, in a local newspaper, and in *The Chronicle of Philanthropy*. In recent years, online job banks, such as the one CASE offers, have made position announcements accessible to a worldwide audience. Although ads are expensive, they do cast a wide net—one that can be very important to school heads with only a few months to fill a key job.

The ideal time to begin a search is at the start of a calendar year. Most development directors have contracts that cover an academic year. It is easiest to attract experienced candidates if they can look for a new job in the winter and spring while they complete an academic year at their current institution.

Once applications arrive and five to 10 top candidates emerge, the next step is to interview with care. Although the school head should have the final say about a new development director, most heads ask others to assess final candidates during school visits. For example, the board chair, the capital campaign chair, the alumni association head, the business manager, a teacher, and a loyal volunteer often form a search committee to interview candidates. Three to four finalists should also meet with every member of the development office staff. Each interviewer should fill out a candidate-evaluation form to help with the decision making. (See a sample on page 107.)

Too often, schools rush through the last important step: meticulous reference checks. Conversations with those who know the candidates should be probing, candid, and clear. During the check, the caller should ask each reference the applicant provides to give the name of someone else who can also evaluate the candidate. Failing to check thoroughly may well lead to a poor choice for the school.

SETTING THE STAGE FOR SUCCESS
Both parties should tackle challenging questions well before the contract is signed.

To avoid misunderstandings on the job, schools should put candor before contracts. During pre-contract conversations, a potential director of development and school head should explore the following questions of mutual concern.

- *Will the development director teach?* Teaching or coaching is often rewarding, and it may help a new development director get to know the school better. However, teaching takes time away from development tasks and may be unwise during a fund raiser's first year or during a capital campaign.
- *Will the development director grow professionally on the job?* Development directors should know in advance if they will have the money and time to attend professional conferences and to purchase relevant books, periodicals, and tapes.
- *What will the development director's priorities be for the upcoming year?* Many school heads give their development directors a list of 10 priorities, listed in order of importance, for each school year.
- *What personnel problems might the development director find?* It is best to speak honestly but confidentially about the strengths and weaknesses of the development staff as well as other administrators and key volunteers.
- *Who will evaluate the development director and when?* Every school head should promise the development director an annual evaluation, first in person and then in a written report.

Beyond exploring those questions, the school head and development director should each make their expectations explicit about working together on a day-to-day basis. To lay the groundwork for a mutually supportive relationship, a school head might agree to:

- Set clear development program priorities for each school year.
- Meet privately with the development director each week.
- Invite the development director to board meetings.
- Include the development director in senior staff meetings.
- Invite the development director to a faculty meeting each fall so that he or she can explain the development program and goals.
- Let the development director manage his or her own time as much and as often as possible.

In return, a new development director might pledge to:

- Respect the school head's busy schedule and to try to use his or her fund-raising time wisely and well.
- Prepare the school head fully, both orally and with written memoranda, for meetings with major prospects and key fund-raising groups.
- Provide timely drafts of gift acknowledgment and stewardship letters for the school head to sign.
- Share rumors or concerns that emerge.
- Manage budget and staff competently.
- Set high personal and professional standards.
- Work cooperatively with other administrators and be sensitive and responsive to their differing points of view.

Off to a Good Start

It is always exciting to begin a new job. For an independent school development director, it can be overwhelming as well. During the initial weeks, a new director of development should remember that:

- Learning about the school must come first. Each school has its own history, culture, climate, morés, and traditions that a new person must understand before fund-raising programs can succeed.

- Relationship building should begin at once. It's important to establish good rapport with colleagues among the administration, fund-raising trustees, and volunteer leaders from the start. Their understanding and support are vital.

- Conferring with other development directors can help. It's useful to visit nearby independent schools and to meet development office peers. They know the city and are sensitive to relevant educational and fund-raising issues. It's rare to find a development director who isn't delighted to help in this way.

- Managing time well is essential. A new job provides a new leaf, an opportunity to work in more efficient ways.

A CHALLENGE AND A JOY

The new director of development is on the job. Many of his "bosses" drop in during the first week to share advice. These visitors include the board chair, the development committee chair, the capital campaign chair, the annual giving chair, the alumni association president, the parents association president, the auction chair, and the homecoming chair.

"Keep smiling," the school head advises. "I am your real boss. But you must have a good relationship with all these other people who give you direction and advice."

The new director of development does keep smiling. He discovers that his job is a challenge and a joy. Independent schools are high-quality, value-oriented, nurturing institutions providing leaders for the new millennium. Their case for support is appealing. They are worthy of generous support, and seeking it is a rewarding endeavor.

Development directors have wonderful opportunities to be creative, to get to know interesting people, and to feel the warm satisfaction of helping their schools prosper.

The school head is pleased as well because she knows that a talented development officer is a colleague to be treasured. Here's advice from one experienced head:

> "Development directors know better than anyone else the importance of thanks. They are the ones who make sure that donors and volunteers get frequent and fulsome praise. I try to remember that the development director deserves, needs, and values thanks as well. Ample appreciation from the boss goes a very long way."

THE REYNOLDS SCHOOL

SAMPLE DEVELOPMENT DIRECTOR SEARCH LETTER

Date

Dear School Head or Development Director by Name,

The Reynolds School has begun to search for a new Director of Development. The position, a description of which is enclosed, will be available on July 1.

I would be most appreciative of your assistance in our search. If you know anyone who meets our qualifications and who may be interested in a challenging and responsible career at a school with remarkable development potential, please ask him or her to contact me directly. In addition, please feel free to post this job notice in an appropriate place at your school so that your colleagues can recommend candidates as well.

Clearly, it is through this type of networking that many competent Development Directors find new positions. For that reason, I would be particularly grateful for your help and delighted to assist you in a similar manner now or in the future.

Best wishes for a happy school year to you and your colleagues.

Sincerely,

_____

Head of School

Enclosure

THE REYNOLDS SCHOOL

EVALUATION FORM FOR DEVELOPMENT DIRECTOR CANDIDATES

Name of Candidate:

Date:

After the interview, please answer as many questions as possible by circling a number 1 through 5. A 1 is the lowest rating; a 5 is the highest.

Oral communication skills	1 2 3 4 5
Written communication skills	1 2 3 4 5
Interpersonal skills	1 2 3 4 5
Organizational skills	1 2 3 4 5
Computer skills	1 2 3 4 5
Experience in staff management	1 2 3 4 5
Experience in working with volunteers	1 2 3 4 5
Expertise in annual fund raising	1 2 3 4 5
Expertise in capital fund raising	1 2 3 4 5
Expertise in planned giving	1 2 3 4 5
Expertise in publications	1 2 3 4 5
Expertise in alumni relations	1 2 3 4 5

Please answer the following questions by circling yes or no.

Would you enjoy working with this candidate?	yes or no
Does this candidate support our school's mission?	yes or no
Would this candidate be comfortable in our community?	yes or no
Would this candidate work well with our board?	yes or no
Would you hire this candidate to work for you in your own professional setting?	yes or no

What appear to be this candidate's primary strengths?

What appear to be this candidate's primary weaknesses?

CHAPTER TEN

POLICIES AND GUIDELINES
GETTING EVERYONE ON THE SAME PAGE

"Having gift policies is a great help to me in my relationship with donors. It means that I can interpret rules rather than make them. It prevents me from being adversarial and lets me be the donor's advocate instead."

—Patricia King Jackson
Director of Development, Sidwell Friends School (DC)

E very independent school should have written policies to guide its development work, staff, and volunteers. From the school's point of view, fund-raising policies document standard practices. They provide everyone involved in annual, capital, or planned giving programs with clear and consistent parameters for the solicitation, the receipt, and the acceptance of all gifts.

From the donor's point of view, fund-raising policies build confidence. Policies demonstrate to donors that the school will manage gifts in a prudent and professional manner and will respond to donors equitably and fairly. Venture philanthropists, in particular, often want to study all school policies before they make a commitment.

Fund-raising policies are intended to:

■ Ensure that the school will handle gifts professionally, acknowledge them promptly, and use them as the donors request.

- Educate the staff and volunteer solicitors.
- Make it clear to everyone who has the final word about gift acceptability and what standards that person or committee will apply.
- Emphasize the fact that a school is not required to accept all gifts, especially ones that are inconsistent with its mission and priorities, that may result in a net loss, that come with unacceptable restrictions, or that raise ethical questions.

In substance, length, and detail, fund-raising policies vary significantly from school to school. Some schools have one comprehensive policy covering all aspects of development. Others have several shorter and more specific policy statements. But no matter how detailed or concise the text, or what variations in content individual schools may prefer, the best policies address fund-raising practices; gift categories (including campaign gifts); valuation; management; planned giving; endowment; donor recognition; and ethics.

FUND-RAISING PRACTICES

The following sample policies are standard for most school programs.

- **Activities:** All fund-raising activities, by any school group and for any purpose, must be approved in advance by the director of development, the development committee of the board, or both.
- **Plans:** The director of development, in cooperation with the school head and development committee chair, will provide a written fund-raising plan for each academic year.
- **Evaluation:** The director of development, school head, and development committee chair will formally evaluate the development program annually.
- **Governance:** Each trustee will play an active, individually designed role in the development program, to be determined annually in consultation with the board chair. The school will make clear its expectations regarding trustee fund raising and personal philanthropy during the recruitment process.
- **Volunteers:** The school will provide written job descriptions to all fund-raising volunteers who are considering service on the development committee; annual, capital, or planned giving committees; alumni committees; or special event committees. Every year, the school will also invite volunteers to evaluate their volunteer efforts and the school's service to its volunteers.

GIFT CATEGORIES

Gift policies guide and document a school's handling of different categories of gifts.

Every school seeks and receives many different kinds of gifts. Therefore, it is important to distinguish categories of gifts and to document the distinctions in writing. The following is a sampling of gift categories and their uses.

- **Unrestricted gifts:** A school may use unrestricted capital gifts when it wishes and as it wishes. It expends unrestricted annual gifts for current operations within a particular academic year. If annual gifts are for a "family of funds," the school may invite donors to designate particular programs or activities they want to support (such as arts, athletics, etc.). However, the school always uses the resulting annual gifts for a purpose that (a) has already been designated by the board as an annual operating expense and (b) is already included in the annual operating budget.

- **Restricted gifts:** A restricted gift, whose purpose is designated by the donor, is acceptable provided it is consistent with the school's mission, goals, and priorities. Restricted gifts are segregated for accounting purposes and may be used only for the designated purpose.

- **Gifts in kind:** Acceptable gifts of tangible personal property should be in good condition and either useful to the school in its educational program or readily salable. It is the donor's responsibility to place a value on the gift for tax purposes. Acceptable gifts of real estate should be readily salable, unmortgaged, and free from environmental hazards or other violations of law.

- **Memorial or tribute gifts:** Gifts in memory or in honor of an individual or family are welcome. The school always notifies the individual or family member remembered or honored.

- **Gifts to name a facility:** The naming of a building requires a gift equal to at least 51 percent of the total construction cost. Should there be future renovations to or replacements of the structure, the original name should be maintained in an appropriate manner.

- **Conditional gifts:** Under the Financial Accounting Standards Board regulations of December 1994, a gift is an unconditional, voluntary, non-reciprocal transfer of assets. If the gift is revocable (as in the case of a will or an insurance policy for which the donor can change the beneficiary at a future date), the school should not record the gift on its books until it receives the gift. If the gift is dependent upon an uncertain future event (as in the case of a challenge that requires matching funds), the school should not record the gift on its books until the precondition has been satisfied.

- **Gifts for a specific campaign:** Policies for capital campaign gifts—including the counting of deferred gifts, the setting of a final goal, guidelines for solicitations and the treatment of annual gifts—are covered in Chapter 7.

GIFT VALUATION

IRS rules for valuing common types of gifts dictate what development officers must do.

Valuation issues are confusing for many development officers. When is a stock gift made? What if it goes up in value before it is sold? Unlike many of the policies in this chapter, valuation rules are regulated by the Internal Revenue Service for donors' tax purposes. The following are IRS rules for valuing common types of gifts.

1. **Marketable securities:** The value of a gift of marketable securities is the average of the high and low quoted selling prices on the date of the gift. If the stock certificate comes by mail, the date of the gift is the date on which it is mailed. If the stock is transferred electronically, its value is established on the day it reaches the school's broker and is beyond the control of the donor.

2. **Closely held stock:** The value of a gift of closely held stock is the fair market value on the date of gift. If the value of the stock exceeds $10,000, a qualified independent appraiser should determine the fair market value.

3. **Real and personal property:** Qualified independent appraisers should value gifts of real or personal property with fair market values exceeding $5,000. The donor may value gifts of personal property under $5,000.

Regulations regarding auction and gala gifts, tickets, and purchases are covered in *Questions and Answers on Gift Substantiation and Quid Pro Quo Disclosure Statement Requirements for Private Schools* by Jefferson Burnett and Donna M. Orem (CASE, NAIS, and the U.S. Catholic Conference, 1994).

GIFT MANAGEMENT

Policies ensure equal treatment of donors and good stewardship of their gifts.

Policies also describe how, when, and by whom gifts and pledge payments will be processed, recorded, and acknowledged. Advance agreement about procedures leads to cooperative efforts and cordial relations between the development and business offices. Most important, it ensures equitable treatment of all donors and appropriate stewardship of all gifts. A sample policy follows.

- **Receipts for gifts:** The school will provide all donors with a written, contemporaneous receipt regardless of the size or purpose of the gift.
- **Acknowledgment of gifts:** The school will thank all donors promptly for

their support. Donors of $1,000 or more will be thanked in writing within two business days. Donors of $25,000 or above will also receive a telephone call from the development director or head of school.

- **Handling of non-cash gifts:** Unless otherwise requested by the donor and approved by the school (usually by a gift-acceptance committee), all marketable securities will be sold upon receipt. Salable gifts in kind that are not useful to the school will be sold as soon as practical.

- **Handling of pledges:** A pledge will be considered a gift to the school only if it is documented in writing with a signature, a specific dollar amount, and a fixed payment schedule. (Note: A pledge, even if legally enforceable, does not provide the donor with an income tax deduction until the year in which the donor pays the pledge.)

- **Stewardship of gifts:** The school will use gifts as donors request and will notify donors in the future if it cannot continue to honor donor intent.

PLANNED GIFT POLICIES
Clear policies can simplify the complexities of planned gifts for donors and staff.

Soliciting and completing a planned gift is often a lengthy process involving philanthropic, personal, tax, and financial considerations for the donor.

Most schools distinguish internally between planned gifts they are likely to accept and those they will market (that is, those they wish to emphasize because they are likely to provide the largest or most immediate benefit to the school).

Planned giving policies typically cover the following:

1. **Planned gift management:** Independent school policies most often state that in no event will the school serve as a trustee or take an active role in the management of a planned gift. Instead, the school may recommend or the donor may choose an institutional manager such as a bank. If the school were to act as a trustee, business offices could be overwhelmed by additional responsibilities, such as investment management and the mailing of periodic income checks to a large number of remainder trust, gift annuity, or pooled income fund donors.

2. **Planned gift menu:** It is important to define clearly which planned gifts are acceptable, under what conditions they are acceptable, and how they will be credited at all times or during a particular campaign. (A sample gift-acceptance policy statement appears on page 116.) Schools that include statements of tax benefits to the donor must be conscientious about updating the text as tax laws change.

3. **Planned gift acceptance:** The acceptance of planned gifts should be the responsibility of a small gift-acceptance committee, usually made up of the school head, development director, board chair, and several others. No matter how well meaning the donors may be, some planned gifts—such as real estate with environmental problems—can be a burden rather than a benefit to a school. All solicitors who discuss planned gifts with potential donors should ask the development director to consult with this committee to ensure that the gift is acceptable and desirable.

ENDOWMENT POLICIES

The finance committee of the board of trustees maintains institutional endowment investment policies. However, a school also needs donor-related endowment policies. The following are typical.

1. **Endowment fund contract:** For all endowment funds established in perpetuity, both the donor and the school will sign an agreement that will include:
   - the name of the donor(s),
   - the initial amount given or pledged,
   - the purpose and the use of the fund,
   - the understanding that the fund's principal can be co-mingled with other endowment for investment purposes, and
   - the understanding that future boards will have the discretion to allocate funds to another closely related purpose if the particular purpose the donor originally designated is no longer acceptable or feasible. (For a sample endowment contract, see page 119.)

2. **Endowment minimums:** The school will set a minimum level (often ranging from $25,000 to $100,000) for permanent endowment funds. Smaller gifts to endowment will be welcomed and will be added directly to appropriate endowment pools.

3. **Endowment pools:** Endowment gifts that are restricted to specific appropriate purposes—such as student financial aid, campus maintenance, or professional development—and that fall below the minimum level for a fund maintained in perpetuity will be put into endowment pools maintained for those purposes.

4. **Named endowment funds:** The school will maintain a list of named endowment fund opportunities and the gift levels required to establish each.

DONOR RECOGNITION

Recognition policies elaborate upon the following topics:

- **Gift societies or gift clubs** established to recognize unrestricted annual gifts.
- **Planned gift societies** for donors who remember the school in an estate plan.
- **Plaques** and other permanent tangible acknowledgments.
- **Annual reports** in which the school publishes donor names. (It is important to preserve anonymity when donors request it.)
- **Named-gift opportunities** for capital projects or endowment. (It is wise to maintain a list of named gift opportunities for interested donors even when a campaign is not in progress.)

ETHICAL GIFT ADMINISTRATION

Chapter 11, which covers 10 principles of fund-raising excellence, outlines the major aspects of the ethical administration of gifts. Every school should provide and publicize board-approved policies regarding ethical fund raising and ensure that everyone follows them conscientiously.

It is particularly important to ensure donors of privacy and confidentiality. Gossip about a large gift, an anonymous gift, a prospect's failure to give, or a prospect's gift potential can do immeasurable harm to an entire development program.

In addition, it is essential to advise donors to consult with their own attorneys and to avoid putting any undue pressure on a potential donor regarding any aspect of the solicitation process.

THE REYNOLDS SCHOOL

GIFT-ACCEPTANCE POLICIES

The following is one school's determination of what gifts it will accept (designated by the letter A) and how it will credit the gift (designated by the letter C). The tax benefits to the donor (designated by the letter B) are established by law and may change over time.* The policies illustrate a useful format; the substance of individual school policies—that is, what they will accept and how they will credit the gifts—may vary.

Gifts of Cash

A The school will accept a gift of cash in any amount.

B The donor will secure an income tax deduction, in the year of the gift, for the amount of the gift.

C The school will give the donor credit for the full amount of the gift.

Gifts of Marketable Securities

A The school will accept a gift of marketable securities in any amount. It is the policy of the school to sell marketable securities upon receipt. Consideration will be given to exceptions for gifts from major stockholders, officers, and directors for whom there may be security law restrictions regarding prompt sale.

B If the donor has held the security for more than one year, the donor will receive an income tax deduction for the value of the security on the date of the gift and will not incur capital gains tax on the excess of that value over the donor's cost basis.

C The school will give the donor credit for the value of the securities on the date of the gift.

Gifts of Remainder Interests

A The school will accept a gift of a remainder, whether transferred by lifetime gift or bequest, and without regard to the age of the income beneficiary, provided that the school has no management responsibility for the period prior to taking possession of the remainder.

---

* *The 2001 Tax Act gradually reduces estate tax rates and increases the estate tax exemption between 2002 and 2009. It fully repeals the estate tax as of January 1, 2010. Furthermore, there is a sunset provision in the 2001 Tax Act that reintroduces the estate tax after a 12-month hiatus, that is, as of January 1, 2011. The foregoing references to the estate tax charitable deduction remain relevant for donors who die prior to 2010.*

B If the gift is made in lifetime, the donor will receive an income tax deduction equal to the actuarial value of the remainder. If the gift is made by will, the donor will receive an estate tax charitable deduction equal to the actuarial value of the remainder.

C The donor will receive credit only for remainder gifts that are irrevocably vested in the school. The school will give the donor credit in the year in which the gift is made for the actuarial value of the remainder.

Gifts of Income Interests

A The school will accept a gift of an income interest provided that there is no management responsibility.

B Generally, the donor will not receive an income tax deduction for a gift of an income interest, but the donor will be able to exclude the income payable to the school, from year to year, from his or her income and thus receive the equivalent of a deduction.

C The school will give the donor credit for the income received in each year of receipt.

Gifts of Real Estate

A The school will accept an outright gift of a home or a remainder gift in a home provided that it has no mortgage. For all proposed real estate gifts, the gift-acceptance committee will be asked to determine that the real estate is immediately salable and that the interim ownership will not create the risk of imposing a liability under federal or state environmental laws.

B In the case of a remainder interest in a home, the donor will get an income tax deduction for the actuarial value of the remainder, if the gift is made in lifetime, and an estate tax charitable deduction for the actuarial value of the remainder, if the gift is made by will. In the case of an outright gift, the income tax deduction or estate tax deduction will be the fair market value.

C The school will give the donor credit for the fair market value of an outright gift and the actuarial value of a remainder gift.

Gifts of Tangible Personal Property

A The school will accept outright gifts of tangible personal property, such as paintings, silver, etc., if either the property is useful in the educational program or if it is readily resalable.

B If the gift is used in the school's educational program, the donor will get an income tax deduction equal to the fair market value. If the gift is accepted for resale, the donor will get an income tax deduction equal to his or her cost (or the value, if less).

C The school will give the donor credit for the appraised value of the gift.

Gifts of Life Insurance

A The school will accept gifts of life insurance policies both when the donor contributes an existing policy and when the donor pays for a new policy to be owned by the school.

B The donor will receive an income tax deduction for the value (or the donor's investment, if less) as opposed to the face amount of the policy, and for the post-gift premium payments.

C The school will give the donor credit for the value (as opposed to the face amount) of an existing policy plus post-gift premium payments.

Qualified Plan Benefits

A The school will accept a post-mortem lump-sum gift of any balance remaining in a qualified plan (IRA, 401(k) plan, pension, or profit-sharing plan).

B The donor will receive an estate tax deduction.

C Qualified plan benefits will be credited when received.

Bequests

A The school will accept bequests, including those (1) for a specific amount or (2) for all or a specified percentage of the donor's residual estate. Bequests may be either outright or contingent.

B The donor may receive an estate tax deduction depending upon the terms of the bequest.

C The school will give the donor, in lifetime, credit for the actuarial value of a bequest if the commitment is non-contingent, capable of valuation, and supported by a legally enforceable agreement. All other bequests will be credited when realized.

THE REYNOLDS SCHOOL
Memorandum of Understanding
To Establish an Endowment Fund

A model of how a school can adjust to meet individual needs and circumstances.

John and Mary Jones wish to establish an endowed fund to provide an annual financial-aid award at The Reynolds School in memory of John's mother, Sara Generous Jones. The following are the terms and conditions for the establishment of the Sara Generous Jones Endowment Fund and for the financial-aid award its income will support.

1. *Name:* The fund shall be called the Sara Generous Jones Endowment Fund (the "Fund"). For purposes of establishing the Fund, John and Mary Jones will contribute $100,000 in four consecutive annual installments of $25,000 each, beginning on February 1, 2002. Additional contributions to the Fund may be added at any time.

2. *Management:* All assets held in the Fund shall be managed by The Reynolds School under guidelines established and reviewed annually by the board of trustees of The Reynolds School. The Fund may be co-mingled with the school's general endowment for purposes of efficient investment. However, the Fund will be segregated for financial-accounting purposes. Unexpended annual income shall be added to the endowment principal. At no time shall the endowment principal (including accumulated income) be expended, except as provided in paragraph 6. [See next page.]

3. *Purpose:* The purpose of the Fund shall be to provide annual financial-aid support for one or two students at The Reynolds School.

4. *Recognition and Acknowledgment:* In order to honor the memory of Sara Generous Jones, to express the appreciation of The Reynolds School to John and Mary Jones, to attract contributions to the Fund from other persons, and to attract funds for similar purposes, acknowledgment in school publications will be provided and publicity in the media will be sought. In addition, an annual report regarding the recipient(s) of the annual award and the disbursement of funds shall be provided for John and Mary Jones as well as other family members whom they may designate.

5. *Administration:* The selection of the annual recipient(s) of the Fund award shall be the responsibility of the head of The Reynolds School or such committee as the head may establish or designate.

6. *Changed Conditions:* In the future, should conditions change so that, in the opinion of the board of trustees of The Reynolds School, it is no longer feasible to provide an annual financial-aid award as outlined in this agreement, the board of trustees shall utilize the principal and income of the Fund for purposes that in its opinion most closely fulfill the intentions of John and Mary Jones as described herein.

7. *Acceptance:* The terms and conditions of this Memorandum of Understanding shall become binding only after it is approved by the board of trustees of The Reynolds School and only after the signatures below have been affixed, as evidenced by the latest date below.

We accept the terms of this Memorandum of Understanding.

_____   _____
John Generous Jones   Date

_____   _____
Mary Jones   Date

_____   _____
President   Date
The Reynolds School Board of Trustees

_____   _____
School Head   Date
The Reynolds School

CHAPTER ELEVEN

MAINTAINING INDEPENDENCE
TEN PRINCIPLES OF FUND-RAISING EXCELLENCE

A business earns its money on its own. The money of the non-profit institution is not its own; it is held in trust for the donors. And the board is the guardian to make sure the money is used for the results for which it has been given.

—Managing the Non-Profit Organization
Peter F. Drucker (HarperBusiness, 1992)

No fund-raising technique is appropriate in every setting. Schools differ in many relevant ways: age, size, location, history, mission, clientele, and culture.

However, some fund-raising principles are appropriate everywhere. They have been tested in many philanthropic settings and over many years.

The following principles of good practice reflect both the best values of the independent school world and the highest standards of fund-raising professionals nationwide. Schools that adopt such principles offer their donors confidence in both the cause and the solicitation process and assure their development officers the respect they deserve.

■ Purpose
The school will use all gifts only for the purposes for which they are sought or given.

■ **Confidentiality**

The school will offer all donors the opportunity to make anonymous gifts. It will also hold all research data regarding prospective donors in confidence.

■ **Disclosure**

The school will disclose annually the total amount of voluntary support it receives, the costs associated with the raising of those funds, and the uses to which the funds have been or will be put.

■ **Leadership**

The school will inform all donors of the names of those serving on the school's board of trustees, those in fund-raising leadership positions, and those in the top administration of the school.

■ **Substitutions**

The school will accept all gifts as voluntary contributions only, not in lieu of tuition or other fees.

■ **Consultations**

The school will encourage donors contemplating planned or deferred gifts to consult with their own attorneys or financial advisers during the decision-making process.

■ **Information**

The school will offer all donors access to its most recent financial statements and to other relevant public information.

■ **Appreciation**

The school will give all donors immediate acknowledgment of and appropriate recognition for their gifts.

■ **Compensation**

The school will hire development staff members and consultants only at pre-arranged set salaries or fees, which will not be contingent upon fund-raising results.

■ **Independence**

The school reserves the right to refuse gifts that detract in any way from its character, integrity, or mission.

CHAPTER TWELVE

TEN MAXIMS THAT MATTER

I do not look upon this job of fund raising as asking for money. I look upon the role I play, and the roles that others who are involved in philanthropy play, as providing opportunities for people to invest in worthy and needed causes which help an institution and which bring satisfaction to the donor that cannot be realized in any other way.

—James Noyes Jr.
Former board chair, Cornell University

Here is this book's most important message for development directors and other professional fund raisers: *Major donors and major gifts should occupy most of your time.*

In light of this vital message, and in closing, here are 10 maxims to inform the quest for major gifts.

1. **Leadership gifts are essential to the success of every fund-raising campaign.** Every fund raiser's first job is to identify, interest, and involve those members of the school community who are willing and able to give major support.

2. **People give to people.** The most effective solicitations are always face-to-face, and the most effective solicitors know the prospect and believe deeply in the cause.

3. **The best prospects are almost always previous donors.** Look first for major donors among those who have already supported your school. The more donors have given in the past, the more they're likely to give now.

4. **Major donors usually make their largest gifts to organizations they serve as trustees.** Therefore, choose new trustees with care. Be sure that many of them are capable of major support.

5. **Donors respond to exciting plans, projects, and ideas more generously than to timetables or goals.** Don't ask prospects to help you meet a target or deadline. Instead, ask them to join you in making an institutional dream come true.

6. **Fund-raising formulas and techniques must be appropriate for your school.** Don't adopt someone else's methods or plans unless they feel right in your climate and culture and seem appropriate at this moment in time.

7. *Set your sights high when you solicit a major gift.* People almost never contribute more than they are asked to give. On the other hand, major gift prospects are rarely offended by a respectful request for a gift they cannot or do not wish to make.

8. **Always bring a major prospect a personal letter summarizing the institutional need and the specific gift request.** For major gift prospects, an individual proposal is an invaluable supplement to the printed case for support.

9. **Every major gift solicitation is, by definition, a success.** A solicitor presents the needs of the school in person to a prospect who can help in a significant way. A refusal today may lead to major gifts in future years. Therefore, no matter what the result, thank the prospect for the opportunity to meet and promise to keep in touch.

10. **You can never say "thank you" too often for generous voluntary support.** Find many different ways to express appreciation. And when soliciting a gift from a previous donor, always say "thank you" before you say "please."

APPENDIX A

RECOMMENDED READING
FOR INDEPENDENT SCHOOL DEVELOPMENT OFFICERS

The following books have informed my work for many years. Some are new; others are older publications to which I still refer; some are out of print but worth reading in libraries. NAIS has made every effort to locate the most recent publishers of each work.—HC

Bancel, Marilyn. *Preparing Your Capital Campaign*. San Francisco, CA: Jossey-Bass, 2000.

Barrett, Richard D. and Molly E. Ware. *Planned Giving Essentials: A Step by Step Guide to Success*. New York, NY: Aspen Publishers, Inc., 1997.

Berendt, Robert J. and J. Richard Taft. *How to Rate Your Development Office: A Fund-Raising Primer for the Chief Executive*. Washington, DC: Taft Group, 1983. (Out of print.)

Buchanan, Peter McE. (Ed.). *Handbook of Institutional Advancement* (3rd edition). Washington, DC: Council for Advancement and Support of Education, 2000.

Burnett, Jefferson G. and Donna M. Orem. *Questions and Answers on Gift Substantiation and Quid Pro Quo Disclosure Statement Requirements for Private Schools*. Washington, DC: Council for Advancement and Support of Education, National Association of Independent Schools, and United States Catholic Conference, 1994.

Ciconte, Barbara Kushner and Jeanne G. Jacob. *Fundraising Basics: A Complete Guide* (2nd edition). New York, NY: Aspen Publishers, Inc., 2001.

Collier, Charles W. *Wealth in Families*. Cambridge, MA: Harvard University, 2001.

Council for Advancement and Support of Education. *CASE Management Reporting Standards: Standards for Annual Giving and Campaigns in Educational Fund Raising*. Washington, DC: Council for Advancement and Support of Education, 1996.

DeKuyper, Mary Hundley. *Trustee Handbook: A Guide to Effective Governance for Independent School Boards* (7th edition). Washington, DC: National Association of Independent Schools, 1998.

Dove, Kent E. *Conducting a Successful Capital Campaign: The New, Revised, and Expanded Edition of the Leading Guide to Plan and Implement a Capital Campaign* (2nd edition). San Francisco, CA: Jossey-Bass, 2001.

Dove, Kent E. *Conducting a Successful Fundraising Program: A Comprehensive Guide and Resource*. San Francisco, CA: Jossey-Bass, 2001

Drucker, Peter F. *Managing the Non-Profit Organization: Principles and Practices*. New York, NY: HarperBusiness, 1992.

Fischer, Marilyn. *Ethical Decision Making in Fund Raising,* New York, NY: John Wiley & Sons, Inc., 2000.

The Foundation Center. *The Foundation Center's Guide to Grantseeking on the Web*: 2000 Edition. New York, NY: The Foundation Center, 2001.

Frantzreb, Arthur C. *Not on This Board You Don't: Making Your Trustees More Effective*. Chicago, IL: Bonus Books, 1997.

Gayley, Henry T. *How to Write for Development*. Washington, DC: Council for Advancement and Support of Education, 1991.

Gooch, Judith Mirick. *Writing Winning Proposals*. Washington, DC: Council for Advancement and Support of Education, 1987. (Out of print.)

Grace, Catherine O'Neill (Ed.). *Marketing Independent Schools in the 21st Century*. Washington, DC: National Association of Independent Schools, 2001.

Grace, Kay Sprinkel. *Beyond Fund Raising: New Strategies for Nonprofit Innovation and Investment*. New York, NY: John Wiley & Sons, Inc., 1997.

Gurin, Maurice G. *Confessions of a Fund Raiser: Lessons of an Instructive Career*. Washington, DC: Taft Group, 1985. (Out of print.)

Howe, Fisher. *Fund-Raising and the Nonprofit Board*. Washington, DC: National Center for Nonprofit Boards, 1998.

Johnston, Michael. *The Fund Raiser's Guide to the Internet*. New York, NY: John Wiley & Sons, Inc., 1998.

Jones, Jeremy (Ed.). *A Development Handbook: Promoting Philanthropy at Independent Schools*. Washington, DC: Council for Advancement and Support of Education, 1992.

Kihlstedt, Andrea and Catherine Schwartz. *Capital Campaigns: Strategies That Work*. New York, NY: Aspen Publishers, Inc., 1997.

Lansdowne, David. *Fund Raising Realities Every Board Member Must Face: A One-Hour Crash Course on Raising Major Gifts for Nonprofit Organizations.* Medfield, MA: Emerson & Church, 1998.

Lord, James Gregory. *The Raising of Money: Thirty-Five Essentials Every Trustee Should Know.* Cleveland, OH: Third Sector Press, 1984.

Matheny, Richard E. *Major Gifts: Solicitation Strategies.* Washington, DC: Council for Advancement and Support of Education, 1999.

Moerschbaecher, Lynda S. *Starting at Square One: Starting and Managing the Planned Gift Program.* Chicago, IL: Bonus Books, 1998.

Muir, Roy and Jerry May (Eds.). *Developing an Effective Major Gift Program: From Managing Staff to Soliciting Gifts.* Washington, DC: Council for Advancement and Support of Education, 1993.

Murray, Dennis J. *The Guaranteed Fund-Raising System: A Systems Approach to Developing Fund-Raising Plans* (2nd edition). Poughkeepsie, NY: American Institute of Management, 1994.

National Center for Nonprofit Boards. *Realities and Rewards of Trusteeship: Board Members and Staff of Nonprofit Organizations Share Their Stories.* Washington, D.C.: National Center for Nonprofit Boards, 1994. (Out of print.)

Nichols, Judith E. *Targeted Fund Raising: Defining and Refining Your Development Strategy.* Chicago, IL: Precept Press, Inc., 1994.

O'Connell, Brian. *America's Voluntary Spirit: A Book of Readings.* New York, NY: The Foundation Center, 1983.

Panas, Jerold. *Finders Keepers: Lessons I've Learned About Dynamic Fundraising.* Chicago, IL: Bonus Books, 1999.

Quigg, H. Gerald (Ed.). *The Successful Capital Campaign: From Planning to Victory Celebration.* Washington, DC: Council for Advancement and Support of Education, 1986.

Schmeling, David G. *Planned Giving for the One Person Development Office: Taking the First Steps* (2nd edition). Wheaton, IL: Deferred Giving Services, 2000. (CD and in print.)

Schneiter, Paul H. and Donald T. Nelson. *The Thirteen Most Common Fund-Raising Mistakes and How to Avoid Them.* Washington, DC: Taft Corporation, 1984. (Out of print.)

Schroeder, Fritz W. *Annual Giving: A Practical Approach.* Washington, DC: Council for Advancement and Support of Education, 2000.

Schrum, Jake B. (Ed.). *A Board's Guide to Comprehensive Campaigns.* Washington, DC: Association of Governing Boards of Universities and Colleges, 2000.

Seymour, Harold J. *Designs for Fund-Raising: Principles, Patterns, Techniques* (2nd edition). Farmington Hills, MI: Taft Group, 1999.

Stone, Susan C. *Shaping Strategy: Independent School Planning in the '90s.* Washington, DC: National Association of Independent Schools, 1993.

Sturtevant, William T. *The Artful Journey: Cultivating and Soliciting the Major Gift.* Chicago, IL: Bonus Books, 1997.

Teitell, Conrad. *Portable Planned Giving Manual* (9th edition). Old Greenwich, CT: Taxwise Giving, 2001.

Tempel, Eugene R. *The Development Committee: Fund Raising Begins with the Board.* Washington, DC: National Center for Nonprofit Boards, 1996.

Verdery, John D. *Dear Chris: Advice to a Volunteer Fund Raiser.* Rockville, MD: Taft Group, 1986.

Warwick, Mal. *How to Write Successful Fundraising Letters.* San Francisco, CA: Jossey-Bass, 2001.

Williams, Karla A. *Donor Focused Strategies for Annual Giving.* New York, NY: Aspen Publishers, Inc., 1997.

Williams, M. Jane. *Big Gifts: How to Maximize Gifts from Individuals, With or Without a Capital Campaign.* Rockville, MD: Taft Group, 1991.

Worth, Michael J. (Ed.). *Educational Fund Raising: Principles and Practice.* Phoenix, AZ: ACE/Oryx Press, 1993.

ABOUT THE AUTHOR

Helen A. Colson, who serves NAIS as its development consultant, is president of Helen Colson Development Associates in Chevy Chase, Maryland, a consulting firm specializing in independent schools. Before establishing her own firm in 1990, she worked for 12 years as associate headmaster for development and planning at the Sidwell Friends School in Washington, DC.

A graduate of Wellesley College, Colson earned a master's degree from the Fletcher School of Law and Diplomacy. She began her career as a journalist and thereafter became a partner in the Washington, DC, fund-raising consulting firm, Writers-At-Large.

Colson has served as a trustee of many educational institutions and is a frequent speaker at NAIS and CASE conferences. In 1990, she received CASE's Robert Bell Crow Award for service to the national independent school community; in 1997, she received CASE's Steuben Apple award for teaching excellence.